DK EYEWITNESS TOP 10 TRAVEL GUIDES

DUBLIN

POLLY PHILLIMORE
&
ANDREW SANGER

Left **Four Courts** Right **Horse and Carriages, Killarney**

LONDON, NEW YORK,
MELBOURNE, MUNICH AND DELHI
www.dk.com

Produced by Sargasso Media Ltd, London

Reproduced by Colourscan, Singapore
Printed and bound in China by Leo Paper
Products Ltd

First American Edition, 2003
06 07 08 09 10 9 8 7 6

Published in the United States by
DK Publishing, Inc., 375 Hudson Street,
New York, New York 10014

ISSN 1479-344X
ISBN 0-7894-9183-4

Within each Top 10 list in this book, no
hierarchy of quality or popularity is implied.
All 10 are, in the editor's opinion, of
roughly equal merit.

Contents

Dublin's Top 10

The information in this DK Eyewitness Top 10 Travel Guide is checked annually.
Every effort has been made to ensure that this book is as up-to-date as possible at the time of
going to press. Some details, however, such as telephone numbers, opening hours, prices,
gallery hanging arrangements and travel information are liable to change. The publishers
cannot accept responsibility for any consequences arising from the use of this book, nor for
any material on third party websites, and cannot guarantee that any website address in this
book will be a suitable source of travel information. We value the views and suggestions of
our readers very highly. Please write to: Publisher, DK Eyewitness Travel Guides,
Dorling Kindersley, 80 Strand, London, Great Britain WC2R 0RL.

Left **Glendalough** Right **Rock of Dunamase**

Left **Powerscourt Gardens** Right **Grafton Street**

Key to abbreviations
Adm *admission charge*   **Free** *no admission charge*   **Dis. access** *disabled access*

DUBLIN'S TOP10

DUBLIN'S TOP 10

🔟 Dublin's Highlights

One of the most popular capitals in Europe, Dublin is a city steeped in history. Huddled together within a small vicinity you'll find Viking remains, medieval cathedrals and churches, Georgian squares and excellent museums. But it's not just about buildings – music, theatre, literature and pubs play just as strong a part in Dublin's atmosphere. These 10 sights are the must-sees for any visitor who wants to truly capture the variety and vibrancy of the city.

Trinity College 1
The elder statesman of Ireland's universities, Trinity is also one of the oldest in Europe. Its buildings and grounds are a landmark in the heart of the city *(see pp8–9)*.

National Museum of Ireland 2
Three collections in three locations make up this outstanding museum, ranging from dinosaurs to modern furniture *(see pp10–11)*.

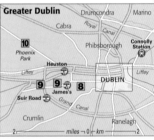

National Gallery 3
Wonderful Italian, French, Dutch and Spanish works are exhibited here, alongside an impressive collection of Irish art *(see pp12–13)*.

Dublin Castle 4
A surprisingly peaceful area, the castle was built into the medieval walls of the city and originally protected by the River Liffey to the north and the now underground River Poddle *(see pp14–17)*.

Christ Church Cathedral 6
Striking Norman, Gothic, Romanesque and Victorian features jostle for attention in this former Viking church (see pp20–21).

Temple Bar 5
This ancient part of the city has been revamped into one of the busiest areas, day and night. There is no shortage of places to eat and drink (see pp18–19).

St Patrick's Cathedral 7
Known colloquially as the "People's Cathedral", this is one of the earliest Christian sites in the city and is the Protestant community's main place of worship in the capital (see pp22–3).

Guinness Storehouse 8
A pint of Guinness could be the country's national symbol. This fascinating exhibition at the Guinness Brewery ends with a welcome free pint of the famous black stuff in the sampling bar (see pp24–5).

Kilmainham Gaol and Kilmainham Hospital 9
After a sobering tour of the one-time prison, lighten the mood at the former hospital, which now houses the Irish Museum of Modern Art (see pp26–7).

Phoenix Park 10
The great pride and play area of Dubliners, this is the largest city park in Europe. Historic monuments and Dublin Zoo are only a few of its delights (see pp28–9).

TOP 10 Trinity College

Trinity College is Dublin's most famous educational institution and, since its foundation in the 16th century, has produced many impressive alumni, among them Jonathan Swift, William Congreve, Oliver Goldsmith, Oscar Wilde, Bram Stoker and Samuel Beckett. Situated on College Green, this was once part of the All Hallows Monastery grounds, but is unfortunately now a busy road junction. It is Trinity itself that provides the haven in this area. Entering through the West Front, under a wooden-tiled archway, is like walking into a bucolic time-warp: cobbled quadrangle, smooth green lawns and an array of fine 18th- and 19th-century buildings. A number of the buildings are open to the public, the most outstanding being the Old Library, home to more than 4 million books and one of the country's greatest treasures, the Book of Kells.

Façade

🅐 In South Frederick Street there's an excellent Italian delicatessen serving delicious snacks, wine and coffee.

🅒 The exhibition "The Book of Kells: Turning Darkness into Light" explains the history and background to illuminated manuscripts. It includes full-scale reproductions of the Book of Kells and a number of others.

- *College Green*
- *Map F4*
- *01-608 2308*
- *www.tcd.ie*
- *Library open Jun–Sep: 9:30am–5pm Mon–Sat, 9:30am–4:30pm Sun; Oct–May: 9:30am–5pm Mon–Sat, noon–4:30pm Sun*
- *Adm €7.50*
- *Dis. access*

Top 10 Features

1. West Front
2. Campanile
3. Old Library
4. Book of Kells
5. Examination Hall
6. Chapel
7. Dining Hall
8. Museum Building
9. Berkeley Library Building
10. Douglas Hyde Gallery

1 West Front

College Green, facing the West Front entrance to Trinity, was originally called Hoggen Green. The statues of Edmund Burke and Oliver Goldsmith which flank the entrance are the work of the sculptor John Foley.

2 Campanile

This 30-m (100-ft) bell-tower *(right)* is the centrepiece of Trinity's main quad, enclosed by fine 18th- and 19th-century buildings. Built by Sir Charles Lanyon, the architect of Queen's University in Belfast, in 1853, it marks the site of All Hallows monastery.

3 Old Library

Entry to the Old Library *(above)*, built between 1712 and 1732, is from Fellows' Square. The finest feature is the magnificent 64-m (200-ft) Long Room, with two tiers of antiquated oak bookcases holding more than 200,000 books. The barrel-vaulted ceiling was added in 1860. The collection grows yearly as Trinity is entitled to copies of all titles published in Ireland and the UK.

For more historic buildings in Dublin See pp32–3

4 Book Of Kells

This beautifully decorated illuminated manuscript is one of the city's most treasured possessions. It is thought to date from around AD 800 and is believed to be the work of monks from the island of Iona in Scotland. They moved to Kells in County Meath to escape Viking raids and the book was eventually given to Trinity by the Bishop of Meath in 1654.

Plan of Trinity College

5 Examination Hall

Both the hall and the chapel were designed by the Scottish architect Sir William Chambers in the 1780s. The most memorable feature is the gilded oak chandelier.

6 Chapel

The chapel, completed in 1798, is the only one in Ireland shared by all denominations. The fine stained-glass window *(right)* above the altar dates from 1867.

7 Dining Hall

Just beside the chapel, this grand dining hall, where Trinity's many students eat, was originally built by Richard Cassels in 1742, but it has been considerably altered over the the past 250 years. It has been totally restored after a fire in 1984 and the walls are hung with huge portraits of college dignitaries.

8 Museum Building

This fine Venetian-style building *(above)* was designed by Sir Thomas Deane and Benjamin Woodward and completed in 1857. Inside, a pair of giant Irish deer skeletons stand guard in the magnificent hall. The detailed decoration of smaller animals, birds and flowers was carved by the O'Shea brothers.

9 Berkeley Library Building

In front of Paul Koralek's 1967 creation is the sculpture *Sphere within a Sphere* (1982) by Arnaldo Pomodoro *(below)*.

10 Douglas Hyde Gallery

One of Ireland's leading contemporary art galleries, the Douglas Hyde has exhibitions by both emerging and well-established artists from Ireland and abroad.

The History of Trinity College

Founded in 1592 by Queen Elizabeth I on the site of All Hallows Augustinian Monastery, and modelled on the universities of Oxford and Cambridge, Trinity's objective was to provide young Protestants with an alternative to going to universities in Europe where they might fall under the influence of Catholicism. The Anglican bias lasted into the 1970s even though religious restrictions were abolished in 1793.

🔟 National Museum of Ireland

There are three different parts to this huge and outstanding museum. The Kildare Street branch offers archaeology and history, ranging from prehistoric Ireland's early culture to the fierce conflict of 1916–22 (see p35) portrayed in the Road to Independence exhibition. The Merrion Street branch comprises the Museum of Natural History, colloquially known as "The Dead Zoo" – every sort of animal and environmental artifact is displayed over three floors. The third branch of the museum is in Benburb Street, at the west end of the city in the recently converted Collins Barracks. This is a very different experience, with the most up-to-date display techniques and interesting and varied collections portraying the country's decorative arts and social, military, economic and political history.

Museum of Natural History façade

🄲 The café at Collins Barracks is excellent. If the weather's good you can sit out under the arches and admire the courtyard and the buildings.

• National Museum of Ireland: Kildare Street, Dublin 2; National History Museum: Merrion Street, Dublin 2; Collins Barracks: Benburb Street, Dublin 7
• Map F5
• 01-677 7444
• www.museum.ie
• Open 10am–5pm Tue–Sat, 2–5pm Sun
• Free
• Dis. access ground floor only (National History Museum); partial (Collins Barracks)

Top 10 Exhibits

1. Façade
2. Or – Ireland's Gold
3. Treasury
4. Viking Collection
5. The Road to Independence
6. Prehistoric Ireland
7. Curator's Choice
8. Fonthill Vase
9. Irish Silver
10. Scientific Instruments

Façade
The exterior of the museum in Kildare Street is an example of Neo-Palladian style, recently enhanced by renovation. Enter the grand portals into the foyer with its 19-m (62-ft) domed ceiling and exquisite floor mosaics.

Or – Ireland's Gold
This outstanding collection of ancient gold *(below)* was found in various counties as far apart as County Clare and County Derry. The pieces show the extraordinary level of skill and invention of 7th- and 8th-century artisans.

Treasury
Part of a hoard found in County Limerick in 1868, the Ardagh Chalice is probably the museum's most famous object. The superbly crafted mid-8th-century ministerial chalice is a beautiful example of the Irish Early Christian metalworker's craft. Another beauty from this great collection is the Tara Brooch.

4 Viking Collection
Ireland's Viking Age spanned from AD 800–1200 and part of this exhibition *(above)* concentrates on the warlike aspect of this period. The skeleton of a warrior complete with sword was excavated from burial grounds around Kilmainham *(see pp26–7)*.

5 The Road to Independence
An important section of the museum for anyone trying to get a grasp of Ireland's history at the time of independence. The events, casualties and repercussions of the 1916–22 struggle are starkly presented *(above)*, and the uniforms of the participants give a sobering touch.

6 Prehistoric Ireland
The Lurgan Longboat, dating from around 2500 BC, is an extraordinary exhibit, made out of hollowed-out oak trunks and 15 m (50 ft) long. Other interesting pieces include the cast bronze horns, probably played like the Australian didgeridoo, and a range of prehistoric pots *(below)*.

7 Curator's Choice
In this wonderful gallery 25 objects have been selected by respective curators from various collections, each piece displayed to reflect its character and context. The 13th-century carved oak statue of St Molaise from County Sligo and the 19th-century Flora tapestry are just two of the eclectic gathering.

8 Fonthill Vase
This vase *(below)* is of immense significance as the only surviving example of porcelain to have left China in the 14th century and whose history can be traced from that moment on.

9 Irish Silver
The silver collection ranges from the 17th to 20th centuries and shows a huge variety of styles. The arrival of French Huguenot silversmiths in Dublin had a strong influence on local design.

10 Scientific Instruments
Even if you're not of scientific bent you cannot but admire the beauty and precision of these instruments *(below)*. The incredible detail and design of the Astrolabe from the Czech Republic makes it both a fine technical instrument and a work of art.

Museum Guide
If you want to visit all three parts of the National Museum on the same day, start with the Natural History Museum in Merrion Square. The National Museum is only a few minutes' walk from here but there is a tourist Hop-On-Hop-Off bus that will take you from one to the other. If you're walking, turn right at the lights on Baggot Street. Walk along the north side of St Stephen's Green, turn right into Kildare Street to the National Museum. From here to the third wing, Collins Barracks, take the tourist bus to the north of the river.

🔟 National Gallery

The National Gallery's outstanding collection of Western European art ranges from the Middle Ages to the present day and includes, as one might expect in the nation's capital, the most important gathering of Irish art in the world. The gallery was designed by architect Francis Fowke (1823–65) and opened in January 1864. The Milltown Wing was added in 1903, the Beit Wing in 1968 and the Millennium Wing in 2002, the latter bringing a huge improvement in exhibition space and public facilities. The gallery has had some important donors during its history, including Countess Milltown, George Bernard Shaw (see p34), Sir Hugh Lane, Chester Beatty (see p17) and Sir Alfred and Lady Beit. The Beits' remarkable presentation was 17 Dutch, Spanish and British Old Master paintings, including works by Gainsborough, Vermeer and Velázquez.

Façade

🍴 The gallery's Fitzers restaurant is well respected but can get very busy at lunchtime, as it is a popular venue for the local workforce as well as gallery visitors. There is a large open-plan space at the Clare Street entrance which is the self-service restaurant. On the upper level is a café.

• Clare St & Merrion Square, Dublin 2
• Map G5
• 01-661 5133
• www.nationalgallery.ie
• Open 9:30am–5:30pm Mon–Wed, Fri–Sat, 9:30am–8:30pm Thu, noon–5:30pm Sun
• Dis. access
• Free

Top 10 Collections

1. Yeats Museum
2. Irish Art
3. British School
4. Italian Painting
5. French Painting
6. German, Dutch and Flemish Painting
7. Spanish Painting
8. Baroque Rooms
9. The Shaw Room
10. The Millennium Wing

1 Yeats Museum
This exceptional collection includes portraits of the Yeats family as well as an impressive group of Jack B Yeats's paintings, from early favourites such as *The Liffey Swim* (1923) *(below)* to later expressionistic work such as *Grief* (1951).

2 Irish Art
Seven rooms do justice to this extensive collection devoted to 18th- and 19th-century Irish art. Works by Nathaniel Hone the Elder *(above)* are representative of the 18th century, while Nathaniel Hone the Younger begins the transition to the Impressionists, represented by Roderic O'Connor and Walter Frederick Osborne.

3 British School

Paintings in this school span from the Tudor period to the early 20th century with a particularly good 18th-century section. Hogarth, Reynolds, Romney, Gainsborough and Raeburn are particularly well represented.

6 German, Dutch and Flemish Painting

One of the interesting paintings in the Flemish collection is a collaborative work, *Christ in the House of Martha and Mary* (1628), with figures by Peter Paul Rubens set in a Jan Brueghel II landscape *(below)*.

7 Spanish Painting

Goya, Velázquez and Murillo are among many great artists in this collection, which concentrates on the 17th century. The modern era is represented by Picasso's *Still Life with Mandolin* (1924).

8 Baroque Rooms

The Baroque collection is divided in two parts. Room 44 has the Baroque Italian, Spanish, French and Flemish paintings from the 17th and 18th centuries. Room 26 is a gallery devoted to the whole Baroque age in Italy.

4 Italian Painting

The lovely Italian collection ranges from the Renaissance to the 18th century. Caravaggio's *The Taking of Christ* (1602) is the most outstanding piece in the 17th-century works of art.

5 French Painting

Monet's *A River Scene, Autumn* (1874) *(right)* is one of the highlights of the French collection, most of which dates from the 17th to the 19th centuries.

9 The Shaw Room

The financial input from Shaw's estate has enabled the gallery to extend its collections and facilities over the years. This elegant room is lined with portraits of dignitaries, as well as *The Marriage of Strongbow and Aoife (above)* by Daniel Maclise (1854).

10 The Millennium Wing

The main galleries added at the first level of this wing concentrate on modern Irish art, showing the rise of Modernism (rooms 1–5). On other floors there are study rooms, temporary exhibition areas and audio-visual facilities. It is a magnificent addition flooded with light.

Gallery Guide

The National Gallery is made up of four wings on four levels: the Dargan Wing, the Milltown Wing, the Beit Wing and the Millennium Wing. Each wing has colour-coded signs to help visitors find their way around. There is an entrance on Clare Street which is on the same level as the basement of the older building. The Merrion Square entrance matches up with Level One of the Millennium Wing. There are facilities for wheelchair users and a special floor plan, "Green, marked Access", shows the location of all the lifts and ramps.

Dublin's Top 10

13

TOP 10 Dublin Castle

The appropriately imposing structure of Dublin Castle was a controversial symbol of British rule for 700 years, until it was formally handed over to Michael Collins and the Irish Free State in 1922 (see p31). Commissioned by King John in the 13th century, over the years the castle evolved from a medieval fortress into a vice-regal court and administrative centre. It has suffered numerous tribulations in its history, but the most concerted attack was in 1534, when it was besieged by "Silken Thomas" Fitzgerald (so called for his finely embroidered wardrobe), a rebellious courtier who had renounced his allegiance to the English Crown. Its current use is primarily ceremonial. Visitors can tour the ornate state apartments and wander freely around the courtyards and museums.

Façade

🍴 The Silk Road Café beside the Chester Beatty Library has a great setting and serves dishes inspired by the countries featured in the library's collections.

🕐 The state apartments are closed to the public when a foreign dignitary is visiting or a national ceremonial is taking place, so check in advance.

• Dame Street, Dublin 2
• Map D4
• 01-677 7129
• www.dublincastle.ie
• Castle: open 10am–5pm Mon–Fri, 2–5pm Sat–Sun; Chester Beatty Library: open May–Sep: 10am–5pm Mon–Fri, 11am–5pm Sat, 1–5pm Sun; Oct–Apr: 10am–5pm Tue–Fri
• Dis. access
• Free (guided tour of state apartments: Adm €4.50)

Top 10 Features

1. Chester Beatty Library and Gallery
2. Figure of Justice
3. Bedford Tower
4. Chapel Royal
5. Viking Undercroft
6. Throne Room
7. Bermingham Tower Room
8. St Patrick's Hall
9. Gardens
10. Garda Siochana Museum

1 The Chester Beatty Library and Gallery
Sir Alfred Chester Beatty's collection of Oriental art – one of the finest in the world – was moved to these specially designed galleries in 1999 (see pp16–17).

2 Figure of Justice
Approaching the castle from Cork Hill, the Figure of Justice *(above)* guards the main entrance. It faces the Upper Yard, turning its back on the city – as Dubliners cynically commented, an apt symbol of British justice.

3 The Bedford Tower
The Norman gate of the original castle is the base for this attractive 18th-century clock tower *(below)*. In 1907, the Irish "Crown Jewels" – a diamond St Patrick Star and Badge – were stolen from here and never recovered.

The Chapel Royal
4 The exterior of this Neo-Gothic delight is decorated with more than 100 heads beautifully carved out of Tullamore limestone.

Viking Undercroft
5 Medieval excavations show the remains of the original castle, including part of the 9th-century city wall and the moat on the river Poddle.

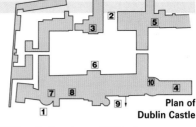

Plan of Dublin Castle

Bermingham Tower Room
7 This former medieval prison was converted into a state apartment.

Gardens
9 To the back of the chapel are the castle's small gardens. The symmetrical design and flowerbeds are often offset by the works of contemporary Irish artists.

Garda Siochana Museum
10 This sombre museum *(above)* is situated in the Record Tower, the only standing remains of the old castle. It offers a comprehensive history of Ireland's police force.

St Patrick's Hall
8 The hall, dedicated to Ireland's patron saint *(below)*, has ceiling paintings by Vincenzo Valdre depicting incidents in British and Irish history, such St Patrick lighting the Pascal Fire on the Hill of Slane.

Building Dublin Castle

In 1204, 30 years after the Anglo-Norman landing in Ireland, King John ordered a castle to be built in Dublin. The site found was the highest ground south-east of the existing town and protected on the east and south side by what was once the River Poddle. Much of this medieval castle was destroyed by fire in 1684 and Sir William Robinson completed the new apartments by 1688. Again, most of these were replaced in the 18th century.

The Throne Room
6 As its name suggests, this is the grandest state apartment in the castle. The throne *(above)* is flanked by four roundels and ovals depicting Venus, Jupiter, Juno and Mars. It is attributed to Giambattista Bellucci, an 18th-century Venetian artist.

Left **Qur'an** Right **Japanese woodblock print**

🔟 Chester Beatty Library Exhibits

1 The Qur'an Collection
This gathering of more than 260 Qur'ans and Qur'an fragments is considered to be the most important of its kind outside the Middle East. Ibn al-Bawwab is reputed to be one of the greatest medieval Islamic calligraphers and displayed here is the exquisite Qur'an he copied in Baghdad in AD 1001.

2 Illuminated Manuscripts
Fine illuminated manuscripts can be found throughout the library, but the copy of the *Gulistan of Sa'di*, made in the 1420s for Baysunghur, a prince of the Timurid dynasty that ruled much of Iran in the 15th century, is one of the most beautiful.

3 Mughal Indian Collection
This collection includes some of the best examples of painting produced under the guidance of emperors Akbar, Shah Jahan and Jahangir.

4 Papyrus Texts
Papyrus is an aquatic plant from which ancient Egyptians made writing materials for their documents. One of the finest here is Paul's Letter to the Romans (c.AD 180–200). The hieroglyphic and demotic papyri relate to administrative and burial practices.

5 Japanese Inro
These tiny, intricate boxes were used to store seals and medicines and are reproduced today by some perfumiers.

6 Chinese Collection
This eclectic display includes the world's largest collection of rhinoceros horn cups, and a stunning range of silk dragon robes.

7 Japanese Picture Books
Some of the finest pieces in the Japanese collection are the painted handscrolls and albums of a type known as *Nara Ehon* (Nara picture books).

8 The Persian Poets
For connoisseurs of Persian poetry, Firdawsi, Nizami, Hafiz and Jami are just four of the authors of the 330 manuscripts.

9 Woodblocks
The *ukiyo-e* woodblock prints complement the outstanding set of more than 700 prints known as *surimono*. The *Hyakumanto darani* is an unusual Buddhist charm housed in a wood stupa.

10 Bust of Chester Beatty
A bust of Chester Beatty by the sculptor Carolyn Mulholland is the centrepiece of a display dedicated to Beatty.

Chinese dragon robe

Top 10 Manuscripts

1. Paul's Letter to the Romans c.AD 180–200 (Western collection)
2. Illuminated initial H, c.1150 *Walsingham Bible*, (Western collection)
3. The Iranian King Kay Kavus Attempts to Fly to Heaven, AD 1480, *The Book of Kings* (Islamic collection)
4. *A Compendium of Military Arts*, AD 1366 (Islamic collection)
5. *Qur'an*, copied by Ibn al-Bawwab, AD 1001 (Islamic collection)
6. *The Story of Ying Ying*, late 17th century (East Asian collection)
7. *The Bhagavadgita Ink*, 18th–19th centuries (East Asian collection)
8. Mandala of Mahamaya, "The Great Illusion", 18th–19th centuries (East Asian collection)
9. *The Song of the Jade Bowl*, Emperor Qianlong, AD 1745 (East Asian collection)
10. *Song of Everlasting Sorrow*, early 17th century (East Asian collection)

Alfred Chester Beatty

Alfred Chester Beatty was born in New York in 1875, and spent much of his childhood collecting stamps, minerals and Chinese snuff bottles. In adulthood, with a highly successful mining consultancy as his profession, he could afford to pursue his interests and eventually gathered

Alfred Chester Beatty

together this outstanding collection of Islamic manuscripts, Chinese, Japanese and other Oriental Art. Beatty lived and worked in both New York and London before finally deciding to settle in Dublin in 1950. He built the first library for his precious collection on Shrewsbury Road, which was improved and added to over the years, before finally relocating to Dublin Castle in 2000. Beatty loved Ireland and contributed generously to its many galleries and cultural institutions. In 1957 he became the country's first honorary citizen, and decided that he would leave his library in trust for the benefit of the public. He died in 1968 and, in recognition of his great contribution to Irish life, he was accorded a state funeral – the only private citizen ever to have received such an honour.

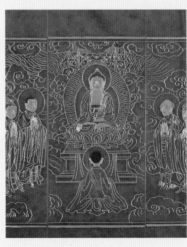

Chinese Jade
This exquisite 18th-century jade book, inlaid with gold and entitled *The Wisdom of Sutra*, is a striking example of Beatty's eye for priceless Far Eastern art.

🔟 Temple Bar

A lively enclave of cafés, bars and theatres, the Temple Bar area covers the network of cobbled streets that stretch between Dame Street and the River Liffey, and from Fishamble Street to Fleet Street. Named after the 17th-century developer Sir William Temple, the area has gone full circle in its fortunes but is now firmly established as the city's most popular spot for tourists and locals alike. Known as Dublin's West Bank, there is something going on here throughout the year, but summer and autumn are definitely the high points. Summer brings "Diversions", a free outdoor cultural event that runs from May to September, while the Dublin Theatre Festival runs for two weeks in the autumn, held in many of the venues around Temple Bar.

City Hall

🔵 Temple Bar is filled with cafés, pubs, restaurants and bars, most of them open from breakfast until after midnight.

🔵 People come into Dublin especially for the Saturday Food Market, which starts at 9:30am and runs until late afternoon, so arrive early for the most choice.

• Map E4
• City Hall: Lord Edward St; Open 10am–5:15pm Mon–Sat, 2–5pm Sun; Adm for exhibition
• Cultivate: 15 Essex St West; Open daily (pm only)
• Gallery of Photography: Meeting House Sq; Open Tue–Sat; Free
• National Photographic Archive: Meeting House Sq; Open Mon–Fri; Free
• Project Arts Centre: 39 Essex St East; Open Mon–Sat; Performances nightly
• Irish Film Institute: 6 Eustace St; Open daily

Top 10 Features
1 City Hall
2 Millennium Bridge
3 Merchant's Arch
4 Meeting House Square
5 Cultivate
6 Cow's Lane
7 Gallery of Photography
8 National Photographic Archive
9 Project Arts Centre
10 Irish Film Institute

City Hall
1 Built by Thomas Cooley between 1769 and 1779, the building was originally designed to be the Royal Exchange, but political events led to a change of usage in the mid-19th century. Built of Portland stone, with a magnificent Rotunda entrance hall, it is an outstanding example of Neo-Classical style *(see p54)*.

Millennium Bridge
2 Only the second pedestrian bridge to cross the Liffey, its simple lines perfectly complement its more famous and more ornate companion, the Ha'penny Bridge *(see p56)*. Designed by architects Howley Harrington, the bridge is intended to increase links between shopping areas north and south of the Liffey.

Merchant's Arch
3 A formal entry point to the area, the arch *(below)* dates from the days when ships sailed right up the Liffey to dock and trade here with the local merchants.

Plan of Temple Bar

4 Meeting House Square

Named after a Quaker Meeting Hall, this is the centre of Temple Bar. It is the venue for concerts, outdoor film screenings, and the Saturday food market *(above)*. Café tables, spilling out onto the street from minute interiors, all add to the atmosphere.

Cow's Lane 6

This smart pedestrian street *(right)* has designer boutiques and chic coffee bars. A Saturday market here sells Irish design and fashion items. (In winter, stalls are in the church at the end of the street.)

9 Project Arts Centre

This modern art centre, begun in 1966 as an artist-led co-operative, has gained an international reputation for avant-garde theatre, dance, music, film and art *(see p41)*.

10 Irish Film Institute

Housing the offices of independent film organizations, a lively bar and restaurant, and two screens, the IFI was one of the first major cultural projects in Temple Bar. The eclectic program focuses on cult and international film.

5 Cultivate

Temple Bar, the site of Ireland's first urban "Green Building", is an innovative centre of eco-design and green lifestyle. Typical of this ethos is Cultivate, a sustainable living centre with a fair trade shop, bookshop café and busy calendar of events. In April/May, they host the Convergence festival with film, exhibits, theatre and talks by leading environmental thinkers. A "green map" of Temple Bar is available at www.sustainable.ie.

7 Gallery of Photography

This bright, contemporary space runs excellent exhibitions by Irish and international photographers. The shop stocks an impressive selection of photo books.

8 National Photographic Archive

This archive houses more than 300,000 photographs from the National Library. The changing exhibitions range from social and political history, to landscapes and postcards.

Regeneration

Sir William Temple bought this land for development in the 1600s and set about reclaiming the marshland to bring trade to the centre. The area thrived for a while, but with the development of the docks to the east, business began to decline. In the 1960s traders made use of the cheap rent and the area took on a Bohemian air. In the 1990s the government regenerated Temple Bar, creating the thriving entity it is today.

🔟 Christ Church Cathedral

The spectacularly imposing cathedral that we see today, towering over its surroundings, is largely a result of 19th-century restoration. Dublin's first church, made of wood, was founded here in 1038 by Sitric Silkenbeard, the first Christian king of the Dublin Norsemen. In 1172, however, Norman Richard de Clare, known as Strongbow, demolished the first church and commissioned his own stone version. The cathedral passed to the Protestant church during the Reformation and, together with St Patrick's Cathedral (see pp22–3), has remained dedicated to the Church of Ireland. Over the last few years the huge crypt has been restored, with new floors and lighting.

Façade

🎵 Concerts are regularly held both in the main body of the cathedral and in the sparkling new crypt, which is particularly atmospheric. Telephone for details.

- Christ Church Place
- Map D4
- 01-677 8099
- www.cccdub.ie
- Open 10am–5pm daily; Closed 26 Dec; Last adm 30 mins before closing
- Partial dis. access
- Adm: cathedral, crypt & treasury €5.00 donation expected. No photography in treasury
- Dublinia: Synod Hall; 01-679 4611; www.dublinia.ie; Open Apr–Sep: 10am–5pm daily, Oct–Mar: 11am–4pm Mon–Sat, 10am–4:30pm Sun; Dis. access; Adm €5.75 (joint ticket for Dublinia and cathedral €8.75)

Top 10 Features

1. Great Nave
2. Strongbow Monument
3. Medieval Lectern
4. Crypt
5. Chapel of St Laud
6. Romanesque Doorway
7. Choir
8. Lord Mayor's Pew
9. Bridge to Synod Hall
10. Lady Chapel

Great Nave
1 The 25-m (80-ft) high nave *(below)* raises the spirits with its fine early Gothic arches. An example of the structural troubles that have beset the cathedral is visible on the north side, where the original 13th-century wall leans out by 50 cm (1.5 ft). This was a result of the collapse of the south wall in 1562.

Strongbow Monument
2 The tomb of the infamous Norman conqueror of Ireland *(above)* is a 14th-century replica and the effigy is not considered to be Strongbow, although it is possible that the fragment beside the tomb may be part of the original. Strongbow's remains are buried in the cathedral.

Medieval Lectern
3 Standing on the left-hand side of the nave in front of the pulpit, this fine brass lectern was handmade during the Middle Ages. There is an identical lectern symmetrically positioned on the south side, but the latter is a 19th-century copy of the original.

Plan of Christ Church Cathedral

4 Crypt
The vast crypt is unusual in that it runs the length of the building. Some pieces are original, but the mummified cat and rat *(above)* have been moved upstairs.

Romanesque Doorway 6
This doorway *(right)* is a fine example of 12th-century Irish stonework. The carvings on the capitals depict a musical troupe.

9 Bridge to Synod Hall
This ornate Gothic bridge was added during the rebuilding of the cathedral in the 1870s. Synod Hall is home to Dublinia, a well-presented re-creation of medieval Dublin *(see p56)*.

10 Lady Chapel
One of the other chapels opening off the central choir area is used to celebrate the daily Eucharist and provides a more intimate setting than the cathedral when numbers are small.

5 Chapel of St Laud
This chapel, one of three extending off the choir, is named after the 5th-century Normandy Bishop of Coutances. The most interesting piece is the wall casket *(below)* containing the heart of St Laurence O'Toole, patron saint of Dublin.

7 Choir
Positioned strategically at the centre of the church, the Victorian wooden stalls are set out behind the choir. The Archbishop's Throne is set in pride of place, with the stalls for the canons and choristers neatly arranged alongside.

8 Lord Mayor's Pew
Generally known as the Civic Pew, but historically belonging to the Lord Mayor, it is kept in the north aisle, but is moved to the front of the nave when required for ceremonial use. Decorated with a carving of the city, there is also a slot for the civic mace.

Strongbow
In the 12th century the chieftains Dermot MacMurrough and Rory O'Connor decided to look to the English for help in trying to conquer Leinster. Richard de Clare, nicknamed Strongbow, answered the call and arrived in 1169 with his Anglo-Normans. He routed Leinster and conquered Dublin, then affirmed his loyalty to King Henry II. It was the beginning of centuries of English hold over Irish land.

⒑ St Patrick's Cathedral

St Patrick's, the Protestant Church of Ireland's national cathedral and commonly known as the "People's Cathedral", stands on an early Christian site where St Patrick is said to have baptized converts in a well in AD 450. Like Christ Church Cathedral (see pp20–21), the original structure was made of wood and it was not until 1192, when Bishop John Comyn founded St Patrick's, that it was rebuilt in stone. Archbishop Henry de Londres restructured it again between 1220 and 1270 and raised its status to that of cathedral. The building has seen its fair share of politics: in 1649, during the Civil War, Cromwell's cavalry used it for stabling; not long after, Huguenot refugees from France sought solace here.

Façade

⏱ Choral evensong is held at 5:45pm every day (3:15pm on Sunday). Sung Eucharist is at 11:15am on Sunday.

Services at Christmas and Easter can be very busy. Early arrival is advised.

- St Patrick's Close, Dublin 2
- Map D5
- 01-453 9472
- Open Mar–Oct: 9am–5:15pm daily; Nov–Feb: 9am–5pm Mon–Sat, 10am–3pm Sun
- Dis. access
- Adm €4.00

Top 10 Features

1. Minot Tower
2. Nave
3. Graves of Jonathan Swift and Stella
4. Boyle Monument
5. Lady Chapel
6. North Transept
7. South Transept
8. Choir
9. South Aisle
10. Wooden Door

❶ Minot Tower
Believed to have been built for defence purposes, the 43-m (140-ft), 14th-century Minot Tower *(above)* still looks out of kilter with the rest of the cathedral.

❷ Nave
St Patrick's is the longest medieval church in Ireland and the nave *(right)* reflects these immense proportions. The pillars are carved with an assortment of figures.

Graves of Jonathan Swift and Stella

One of the first ports of call for many visitors to the cathedral are the graves of Jonathan Swift *(see p34)* and his beloved Stella, positioned beneath the nave beneath brass tablets *(above right)*.

Lady Chapel

At the east end of the church, this 13th-century building was given over to the French Huguenots who arrived as refugees in the mid-17th century. They were given permission to worship here by the Dean and Chapter, and did so for almost 150 years.

North Transept

Flags of Irish Regiments of the British Army are hung in this area and serve to commemorate more than 49,000 Irishmen who died in World War I. In one corner of this transept stands Jonathan Swift's chair, table and pulpit.

South Transept

This former Chapter House boasts a beautiful stained-glass window and, as with all areas of the cathedral, numerous monuments. Particularly interesting is that of Archbishop Marsh which has fine carvings by Grinling Gibbons.

Boyle Monument

The vast monument for the eminent Boyle family *(below)* is overrun with painted figures of the children of Richard Boyle, Earl of Cork.

Choir

Somewhat surprisingly, the choir *(centre)* is adorned with swords, banners and helmets above the pews. These represent the different knights of St Patrick who, until 1869, underwent their services of investiture in this chapel. Another memorial honours Duke Frederick Schomberg, slain during fighting at the Battle of the Boyne *(see p30)*.

South Aisle

Memorials here honour renowned Irish Protestants of the 20th century. Douglas Hyde, Ireland's first president and founder of the Gaelic League is aptly remembered in Irish.

Wooden Door

A row between two 15th-century earls, Kildare and Ormond, reached stalemate when Ormond barricaded himself in the chapter house. Kildare cut a hole in the door *(below)* and offered to shake hands. From this incident came the expression "chancing your arm".

Jonathan Swift

Jonathan Swift was born in Dublin in 1667 and was educated at Trinity College *(see pp8–9)*. In 1694 he took holy orders and, after a year as a curate, moved to England as tutor to Esther Johnson at Moor Park in Surrey. Esther was to become the beloved "Stella" of his writings. Despite a reputation as a wit and pamphleteer, his ecclesiastical career was his primary concern and, in 1713, Swift was appointed dean of St Patrick's. On his death in 1745, he left a legacy of £8,000 to build St Patrick's Hospital for the Insane.

🔟 Guinness Storehouse

Ask the majority of people what they most associate with Ireland, and the likelihood is the answer will be Guinness. Together with whiskey, it is the national drink, famous for its malty flavour and smooth, creamy head. Arthur Guinness founded this immensely successful business in 1759 from relatively humble beginnings but, nearly 250 years on, Guinness is the largest brewery in Europe. The site at St James's Gate covers 64 acres and was unique for having its own water and electricity supply. From here, Guinness exports beer to more than 150 countries worldwide. This extraordinary exhibition covers all aspects of the production, with excellent displays and explanations, before a welcome free pint in one of the bars at the top of the building.

Brewery façade

🍽 The bars on the fifth level sell food as well as Guinness.

🕐 Hold on to your perspex drop of Guinness given to you at the entrance – it doubles up as your ticket and a means to claim your free pint at the end.

The area around the Guinness Storehouse is quite isolated, so the Drop-on-Drop-Off bus is a good option for getting there and back.

- St James's Gate, Dublin 8
- Bus Nos. 51b, 78a, 123
- 01-408 4800
- www.guinness-storehouse.com
- Open 9:30am–5pm, daily; Jul–Aug: 9:30am–9pm
- Dis. access
- Adm €13.50

Top 10 Exhibits

1. Ingredients
2. Brewing Process
3. Arthur Guinness's Study
4. History of Cooperage
5. Transport Gallery
6. Advertising
7. Audiovisual
8. Guinness Abroad
9. Guinness at Home
10. Tasting

1 Ingredients

The tour logically begins with an interactive display about the process of selecting the right ingredients *(below)*. Barley, hops and yeast are displayed in huge barrels and there is a magnified area to see the ingredients close-up, accompanied by a pungent aroma.

2 Brewing Process

This is the noisiest part of the tour. As the machines are mashing, boiling, fermenting, maturing and blending, visitors can watch, smell and hear the entire brewing process in action.

3 Arthur Guinness's Study

This area *(below)* details the setting up of the brewery, what Guinness hoped to achieve and how he went about it. A desk in the corner holds genuine artifacts from his office.

4 History of Cooperage

Cooperage is the process of making and storing casks *(above)*. Films show how the coopers made the old wooden containers – metal casks have been used since the 1950s.

6 Advertising

Here TV and film advertising campaigns run on multi-split screens with the accompanying music, together with a display of all Guinness-associated products and posters *(below)*.

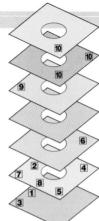

Plan of Guinness Storehouse

9 Guinness at Home

In this interactive exhibit visitors are encouraged to write messages about their love of Guinness.

10 Tasting

Now is the time most visitors wait for – the free pint. There is a choice of three bars; the Gravity Bar *(above)* has magnificent views over the city.

5 Transport Gallery

This display explains all methods of transporting Guinness to suppliers, from the old horse and cart to the sophisticated systems now operating worldwide.

7 Audiovisual

The legendary Irish *craic* – amusing tall stories told over a pint of the black stuff – is enjoyably illustrated in this feel-good audiovisual exhibit *(left)*.

8 Guinness Abroad

Figures are given that 10,000 glasses of Guinness are drunk in 151 countries every day, and a huge glass panel shows what a good time everybody is having.

Arthur Guinness

Arthur Guinness (1725–1803) first bought a lease on a brewery in Leixlip in 1756. Three years later he gave this to his brother when he signed the lease for St James's Gate. He married Olivia Whitmore in 1761, and 10 of their 21 children lived to establish a dynasty that has expanded into many activities worldwide.

🔟 Kilmainham Gaol and Hospital

Despite their communal name, these two sights could not be more contrasting, both in their appearance and history. The forbidding gaol was built in 1789, but the material used was sandstone which wept in bad weather, resulting in damp and grim conditions that adversely affected the health of the inmates. The jail closed in the 1920s and wasn't touched again until it was restored as a museum in the 1960s. Kilmainham Hospital, however, was built in the 1680s as one of Ireland's first Classical-style buildings – Sir William Robinson modelled the hospital on Les Invalides in Paris. It has been home of the Irish Museum of Modern Art since 1991.

Kilmainham Gaol façade

☕ An excellent café in the basement of the IMMA serves good vegetarian and organic dishes.

The hospital grounds are vast, with lovely views, so if the weather is good they are ideal for a picnic.

• Kilmainham Gaol: Inchicore Rd, Dublin 8; Map A4; 01-453 5984; www.heritageireland.ie; Open May–Sep: 9:30am–5pm Mon–Sat, 10am–5pm Sun & public hols; Oct–Apr: 9:30am–4pm Mon–Sat, 10am–5pm Sun & public hols; Adm €5.00
• Kilmainham Hospital & IMMA: Royal Hospital, Military Rd, Dublin 8; Map A4; 01-612 9900; www.modernart.ie; Open 10am–5:30pm Tue–Sat, noon–5:30pm Sun; Dis. access; Free. Some rooms by guided tour only: Jul–Sep, €2.00

Top 10 Features

1. Exhibition
2. West Wing
3. Gaol Chapel
4. East Wing
5. *Asgard*
6. Kilmainham Gate
7. IMMA
8. Gardens & Courtyard
9. Great Hall
10. Hospital Chapel

1 Exhibition
Housed in a modern hall of the gaol, this exhibition puts visitors in the rather gruesome mood for what is to come. On the ground floor is a section on hanging techniques, while upstairs deals with the struggle for independence *(see p31).*

2 West Wing
A fascinating if depressing place *(above)*, it doesn't take much to imagine the horror of internment here. The guide tells of the conditions the prisoners were subjected to – one hour of candlelight a night – and the types of hard labour.

3 Gaol Chapel
The most poignant story related about the chapel *(below)* is the wedding here of Joseph Plunkett and Grace Gifford. They married on the eve of Plunkett's execution, and were allowed 10 minutes alone together before Plunkett was taken out and shot.

4 East Wing
A fine example of the "Panoptical" layout *(below)*, used in many Victorian prisons. The idea was to maximize light but allow for constant surveillance of the prisoners.

5 Tour
A tour covering Irish history from 1796–1924 takes in a children's exercise yard, a Civil War yard, and the Stonebreaker's Yard, in which the leaders of the 1916 uprising were executed *(see p31)*.

6 Kilmainham Gate
This austere doorway *(below)* is flanked by iron gates and sets the mood for a visit to the gaol. A long tree-lined avenue links the fine surroundings of the Kilmainham hospital to its much bleaker neighbour.

7 IMMA
Since its move here in 1991, the Irish Museum of Modern Art (IMMA) *(below)* has made full use of the space available. There is a regularly changing resident collection so even the most regular visitor is likely to see something new. Innovative contemporary art features in touring exhibitions.

8 Gardens and Courtyard
The formal gardens *(left)* of the hospital were designed by Edward Pearce between 1710 and 1720 to represent the crosses of St Andrew and St George. They are currently being restored to their former glory.

9 Great Hall
This grand room served as the soldiers' dining room. The portraits of monarchs and viceroys, commissioned between 1690 and 1734, are the earliest surviving collection of institutional portraits in Ireland.

10 Hospital Chapel
The magnificent ceiling here unfortunately suffered decay at the end of the 19th century and what can now be seen is a *papier mâché* replica of the original. James Tabary, a Huguenot settler, carved the altar, reredos and rails from Irish oak in 1686.

The History of Kilmainham Hospital

Kilmainham's Royal Hospital was built between 1680 and 1686 to the designs of Sir William Robinson, and is considered the most important 17th-century building in Ireland. It was built for single retired veterans. The hospital became a police barracks in 1922 and fell into decline, but was fortunately one of the first buildings to benefit from Dublin's restoration programme in the 1980s. Beautifully renovated, it reopened in 1991 as the IMMA.

🔟 Phoenix Park

Surprisingly for such a small city, Phoenix Park is the largest enclosed urban park in Europe, covering an area of more than 1,750 acres. The name has no connection with the mythical bird but originates from the Gaelic Fionn Uisce which means "clear water" and refers to a spring that once existed here. Following the landscaping traditions of English parkland, complete with hundreds of deer, this is an idyllic place to escape from the bustling city centre. However, there's no shortage of things to do if you want to keep busy.

At the weekends whole families spend the day here, indulging in a variety of activities from dog-walking to jogging, golf practice, hurling matches, charity runs, cricket and polo.

Phoenix Monument

🍺 Ryans, just out of the southeast gate in Parkgate Street, is one of the city's finest pubs both for drink and food.

🛈 Phoenix Park is not considered safe after dark.

• Phoenix Park: Park Gate, Conyngham Rd; Train: Heuston; Open 7am–11pm daily; Free
• Visitor's Centre: 01-677 0095; Open Nov–mid-Mar: 10am–5pm Sat–Sun, mid-Mar–end Mar & Oct: 10am–5:30pm daily, Apr–Sep: 10am–6pm daily; Partial dis. access; Adm €2.75
• Zoo: 01-474 8900; www.dublinzoo.ie; Open Mar–Sep: 9:30am–6pm Mon–Sat 10:30am–6pm Sun, Oct–Feb: 9:30am–dusk Mon–Sat 10:30am–dusk Sun, last adm an hour before closing; Dis. access; Adm €12.50

Top 10 Features

1. Áras an Uachtaráin
2. Phoenix Monument
3. Dublin Zoo
4. People's Garden
5. Papal Cross
6. Wellington Monument
7. Deerfield
8. Visitors' Centre
9. Ashtown Castle
10. Magazine Fort

1 Áras an Uachtaráin
This fine Palladian mansion (1751) by Nathaniel Clements was the vice-regal lodge *(centre)*. In 1937 the lodge became the official home of the Irish president.

2 Phoenix Monument
Lord Chesterfield erected this monument in 1745, topped with what has been described as a poor excuse for a phoenix, looking more like an eagle than the mythical bird.

3 Dublin Zoo
Dublin Zoo *(right)* dates back to 1830 – the second oldest in Europe. The latest addition is the 33-acre "African Plains", providing larger paddocks for rhinoceros, giraffes and antelope *(see p36)*.

4 People's Garden
Close to Park Gate and the Garda Siochana (police) headquarters, this is the only formal area of the park. Decimus Burton landscaped the area in the 1830s and the effect is gentle and restful, as the landscaped hedges and flowerbeds merge with the wilder hillocks and ponds.

5 Papal Cross

The simplicity of the 27-m (90-ft) high stainless steel Papal Cross *(left)* is part of its beauty. It was erected on the spot where Pope John Paul II celebrated Mass in 1979, attended by more than a third of Ireland's population *(see p31)*.

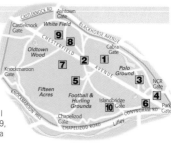

Map of Phoenix Park

10 Magazine Fort

This former fort *(below)* became the main arms depot after independence, but it has been secured and abandoned since the IRA raid in 1939, when more than one million rounds of ammunition were stolen. It is now sadly decaying.

6 Wellington Monument

Designed by Sir William Smirke in 1817, the money given for its construction was used up before it reached 30 m (100 ft). Work resumed in 1861 but the monument *(right)* never realized its original design.

7 Deerfield

This beautiful 18th-century house was once the home of the British Chief Secretary for Ireland, Lord Cavendish, who was murdered in 1882 by an Irish nationalist. It is now the residence of the American ambassador.

8 Visitors' Centre

The display here shows the changing face of Phoenix Park, from 3500 BC to the present day. It also features a reconstruction of the Knockmaree cist grave found in the park in 1838. On Saturday, free tours can be taken to Áras an Uachtaráin from here.

9 Ashtown Castle

A visit to this elegant 17th-century tower house is included in the ticket to the Visitors' Centre. Its claim to fame is that it was once owned by the family of John O'Connell, an ancestor of Daniel O'Connell *(see p31)*. It has cunning features such as a "trip step" on the staircase and a "murder hole" by the door.

The Development of Phoenix Park

In the 16th century, before the Reformation, the land at Phoenix Park belonged to the Knights Hospitallers of St John of Jerusalem. When the Dissolution of the Monasteries demanded the confiscation of all church lands, it became the property of the crown and the Duke of Ormond decided to enclose the land to provide a deer park for Charles II. In the mid-18th century much money was spent on developing Dublin City, including formalizing of the park. It was opened to the public in 1747.

Left **Pope John Paul II delivers mass in Phoenix Park** Right **Battle of the Boyne**

🔟 Moments in History

1 Newgrange
The first settlers arrived in Ireland from the Continent around 4000 BC, bringing with them farming skills and rudimentary tools which allowed them to establish small communities. The megalithic stone tomb of the Neolithic Age at Newgrange *(see p71)* is thought to date from around 3000 BC and is one of the most important passage graves in Europe.

2 Celts Arrive
Powerful tribes of warriors became established in Central Europe around 600 BC. With their ability to produce iron weapons and implements, the Celts were able to progress across the continent to Ireland. Earlier inhabitants remained, but the Celts (or Gaels) imposed their authority, culture and language.

3 Christianity Comes to Ireland
Although the Romans never settled in Ireland it was through them that Christianity reached Irish shores. The first bishop was

Stone tomb, Newgrange

appointed in AD 431 but it is St Patrick *(see p38)* who is credited with the conversion of the pagan Celts and the establishment of the Church between 432 and 461.

4 Viking Ireland
The Vikings arrived in Ireland in the 10th century and established their own communities. In 1030 a wooden church was built where Christ Church Cathedral now stands *(see pp20–21)*.

5 First Irish Parliament
By the 1350s the Normans had settled in Ireland and introduced the feudal system of government, led by a justiciar who was head of the army, the chief judge and top administrator. He was helped in his work by a council of officials, and would occasionally summon a parliament consisting of his council, bishops, abbots and feudal lords. By the end of the 14th century, representatives of counties and towns were part of the process known as the Lower House, or Commons.

6 Battle of the Boyne
After his defeat by William of Orange at the Battle of the Boyne in 1690, James II fled to France leaving Ireland in the hands of the Protestant Ascendancy. These were English descendants of Tudor and Stuart settlers. The native Irish suffered for more than a century from the stringent penal measures inflicted on them.

Georgian High Culture

7 Many of the most important sights in the city, such as Custom House *(see p61)*, were built during the Georgian era. Artists and musicians visited Dublin from all over Europe – one of the highlights was the premiere of Handel's oratorio, *The Messiah*, in Dublin in 1741.

George Frederick Handel

The Great Famine

8 The potato famine dominated 19th-century Ireland. The crop failed first in 1845, then again in 1846–7. Over a million people died of starvation or emigrated in desperation. By 1849 the population had decreased by two million.

The Easter Rising

9 On Easter Monday 1916 Patrick Pearse and others opposed to British rule proclaimed the Declaration of Independence from the General Post Office in O'Connell Street *(see p61)*. An uprising ensued and 15 insurgents were executed. In May 1921 the Anglo-Irish treaty was signed, creating the Irish Free State.

Pope John Paul II

10 In 1979 Pope John Paul II visited Ireland, the high point of which was his mass in Phoenix Park, attended by more than a million people. The Papal Cross marks the spot *(see p29).*

Top 10 Politicians

1 Henry Grattan
Grattan (1746–1820) entered Parliament in 1775 and was a great champion of the Catholic cause.

2 Theobald Wolfe Tone
Tone (1763–98) has been described both as the founder of Irish nationalism and as a frustrated imperialist.

3 Daniel O'Connell
The greatest leader of Catholic Ireland, O'Connell (1775–1847) was a constant agitator against the Union.

4 Charles Stewart Parnell
Leader of the Irish Parliamentary Party in 1880, Parnell (1846–91) secured Gladstone's conversion to Home Rule.

5 Arthur Griffith
Griffith (1871–1922) launched Sinn Fein in 1906 and was elected president of the Dáil in 1922.

6 Patrick Pearse
Pearse (1879–1916) was executed for delivering the Proclamation of Independence in 1916.

7 Michael Collins
Commander-in-Chief of the government forces in the Civil War, Collins (1890–1922) was shot dead in his native County Cork.

8 Eamon de Valera
Valera (1882–1973) was President of the Republic from 1959–73. His political ideal was a 32-county Gaelic republic.

9 Charles Haughey
Prime minister for various terms from 1979 to 1992, Haughey (b.1925) remains a controversial figure.

10 Mary Robinson
Mary Robinson was elected the first woman president in 1990.

Left **Custom House** Right **City Hall**

🔟 Historic Buildings

1 Dublin Castle

Originally rectangular in shape, Dublin Castle was designed as a "keepless castle", involving four circular corner towers and, midway along the south wall, a fifth tower. However, much of the medieval castle was destroyed by fire. The remodelling we see today began at the turn of the 18th century *(see pp14–17)*.

2 Custom House

James Gandon designed the striking Custom House in 1791. There are four decorated façades, with finely balanced end pavilions and recessed Doric columns facing the River Liffey. The exceptional statuary around the building is the work of Edward Smyth. A fire gutted the building in 1921 during the War of Independence, but it was restored in the same decade. The latest superb restoration work was carried out in the 1990s *(see p61)*.

3 Four Courts

West of Custom House is James Gandon's other magnificent edifice. Designed six years earlier in 1785, the Four Courts has a grand pedimented centre with arcaded screens and triumphal arches, topped with a colonnaded rotunda and a Neo-Classical dome. The five statues by Edward Smyth on the central block represent Moses, Wisdom, Authority, Justice and Mercy *(see p66)*.

4 City Hall

A competition was held in 1768 to select the designer of what was then to be the Royal Exchange, and Thomas Cooley's plans were the preferred choice. One of Dublin's most sophisticated Georgian buildings, it marked the introduction to Ireland of the Neo-Classical style of architecture, with its lofty dome supported by 12 columns and its 12 elegant circular windows *(see p54)*.

5 Leinster House

Designed by Richard Cassels in 1745, Leinster House is notable for its two contrasting façades, one resembling a townhouse, the other a country abode. Built for the Earl of Kildare, since 1921 it has been the seat of *Dáil Eireann*, the Irish Parliament *(see p56)*.

Four Courts

6 Bank of Ireland

Built to accommodate the Irish House of Lords and House of Commons, the building is almost as magnificent as its English counterpart. Three architects were involved in its creation: Sir Edward Lovett Pearce designed the Palladian central block, with temple and portico flanked by colonnaded wings, in 1729; James Gandon contributed the portico to the east in 1785; and Richard Parkes added the western Ionic portico. In 1803, the building was taken over by the Bank of Ireland (see p56).

Marsh's Library

7 Marsh's Library

Designed by Sir William Robinson of Kilmainham Hospital fame (see pp26–7) in 1705, this L-shaped library was built to house the collection of Archbishop Narcissus Marsh. The Gothic-style battlements and entrance date from the 19th century, but the oak bookcases, arranged in bays between the windows, are original. ⓢ St Patrick's Close • Map C5 • Open 10am–12:45pm, 2–5pm Mon, Wed–Fri; 10:30am–12:45pm Sat • Adm

8 Rotunda Hospital

Purpose-built as the first maternity hospital in Europe, founded by Dr Bartholomew Mosse in 1745, the building was designed by Richard Cassels. A number of other distinguished architects had a hand in the creation of the adjoining Assembly Rooms, which now comprise a cinema and the Gate Theatre (see p63): John Ensor designed the rotunda in 1764, while the porches were added by Richard Johnston in 1784 and James Gandon in 1786 (see p66).

9 Iveagh House

The first of architect Richard Cassels' notable Dublin houses, sadly the only part that now remains of the original is the first-floor saloon. Sir Benjamin Guinness linked two houses into one in the 1870s. His grandson, the second Earl of Iveagh, later presented the house to the Irish Government. ⓢ St Stephen's Green • Map F6 • Closed to the public

10 Powerscourt Townhouse

This powerful looking building with its grand entrance was designed in 1771 by Robert Mack as a home for the third Viscount Powerscourt. The first-floor reception rooms, by Michael Stapleton, and the elegant hall can still be appreciated even though the house was imaginatively converted into a shopping precinct in 1981 (see p55).

Powerscourt Townhouse

Left **Shaw's Birthplace** Centre **Oscar Wilde statue** Right **James Joyce statue**

Dublin Writers

1 James Joyce

The writer who most prolifically put Dublin on the literary map, Joyce (1882–1941) was born and educated in the city. He met Nora Barnacle on 16 June 1904 and, although they did not marry for 30 years, it became the date for events in his epic work *Ulysses*, published in Paris in 1922. *Dubliners* (1914), *Portrait of the Artist as a Young Man* (1916) and *Finnegan's Wake* (1938) are among his other works.

2 William Butler Yeats

Willliam Butler (1865–1939), brother of the painter Jack B Yeats, was born in Dublin. His first volume of poetry *The Wanderings of Oisin and Other Poems* was well received and later volumes confirmed his status as a leading poet. His play *On Baile's Strand* was chosen for the Abbey Theatre's opening in 1904 *(see p62)*.

3 George Bernard Shaw

Born in Dublin, Shaw (1856–1950) moved to England in 1876. Starting as a book reviewer for the *Pall Mall Gazette*, he was to become a prolific playwright; *The Devil's Disciple* (1897) and *Pygmalion* (1914) are just two of his works. He received the Nobel Prize for Literature in 1925.

George Bernard Shaw bust

4 Jonathan Swift

Swift (1667–1745) was born and educated in Dublin *(see p23)* and established a reputation as a wit through his satirical works. *A Modest Proposal* (1729), one of his most brilliant – if grim – satires, suggested feeding poor children to the rich. It is ironic that his work, *Gulliver's Travels* (1726), is a children's classic.

5 Oscar Wilde

Wilde (1854–1900) was born at Westland Row, Dublin, and became a classics scholar at Trinity College *(see pp8–9)* and later at Oxford. His highly popular plays, full of acid wit, include *An Ideal Husband* (1895) and *The Importance of Being Earnest* (1895). His imprisonment for homosexual offences inspired *The Ballad of Reading Gaol* (1898), but he died, humiliated, in 1900.

6 Sean O'Casey

Dublin-born O'Casey (1880–1964) worked on the railways and became an active trades unionist. He achieved instant success with *The Shadow of a Gunman* (1923), set in the Dublin slums, followed by the play *Juno and the Paycock* in 1924 and his best-known work *The Plough and the Stars* in 1926. His later plays never had the appeal of the early works.

Samuel Beckett

Top 10 Contemporary Irish Writers

1 Seamus Heaney
Ireland's most prominent poet, Heaney (b.1939) won the Nobel Prize for Literature in 1995. *North* (1975) explores the Troubles in Northern Ireland.

2 William Trevor
Trevor (b.1928) is a master of the short story genre.

3 John Banville
The Literary Editor of the *Irish Times*, Banville (b.1945) is also a novelist – *The Book of Evidence* (1989) is one of his finest works.

4 John McGahern
One of McGahern's (b.1934) best novels is *Amongst Women* (1990).

5 Brian Friel
Playwright Friel's (b.1929) successes include *Dancing at Lughnasa* (1990).

6 Roddy Doyle
Renowned for his *Barrytown Trilogy* about Dublin life, Doyle (b.1958) won the Booker Prize in 1994 for *Paddy Clarke Ha Ha Ha!* (1993).

7 Edna O'Brien
The Country Girls (1960) is O'Brien's (b.1930) most well-known novel to date.

8 Colm Toibin
Toibin (b.1955) was short-listed for the 2000 Booker Prize with his novel *Blackwater Lightship* (1999).

9 Frank McCourt
McCourt's (b.1930) evocative account of a poverty-stricken upbringing in Limerick in *Angela's Ashes* (1996) won him the Pulitzer Prize

10 Tom Murphy
A controversial playwright, Murphy's (b.1935) work *The Wake* (1998) had a long run at the Gate Theatre *(see p63)*.

7 Samuel Beckett
French Huguenot by descent, after a distinguished career at Trinity College, Beckett (1906–89) spent much of his life in France. The play *Waiting for Godot* (1952) made him an international name. He received the Nobel Prize for Literature in 1969.

8 Edmund Burke
Burke (1729–97) was born in Dublin, went to Trinity College and then to London to study law. A champion of individual liberty against the monarchy, his *Reflections on the Revolution in France* (1790) established his reputation.

9 Elizabeth Bowen
Although born in Dublin, Elizabeth Bowen (1899–1973) spent much of her childhood in Cork. Her years in London are evoked in her novels, including *The Heat of the Day* (1949).

10 Patrick Kavanagh
Kavanagh (1904–67), born in Monaghan, went to London in 1939 and began a career as a poet and journalist. His reputation was established with a long and bitter poem of rural life, *The Great Hunger* (1942).

Left **Dublin Zoo** Right **Dublinia**

🔟 Children's Attractions

1 The Ark
Workshops, art classes, plays, exhibitions and concerts geared towards children between 4 and 14 years. Book ahead. ◈ *11a Eustace St • Map E4 • 670 7788 • Open 10am–4pm Mon–Fri • Adm*

2 Dublinia
Medieval Dublin is brought to life, through exhibits such as a full-size reconstruction of a merchant's house *(see p56)*.

3 Dublin Zoo
Apart from the usual exotic animals there is a pet-care section, play area, and a train ride *(see pp28–9)*.

4 My Museum
An exciting programme of activities run by the National Museum of Ireland, which rotates between the city's museums. ◈ *677 7444 • Sun pm • www.museum.ie*

5 Viking Splash Tour
A costumed driver gives a lively tour on land in a military amphibious vehicle before splashing into the waters of the Grand Canal Quay. Passengers are encouraged to let out Viking roars. ◈ *Bull Alley St • Map D5 • Open mid-Feb–Nov: daily • Adm*

6 Wax Museum
Small children enjoy "The World of Fairytales and Fantasy"; older children prefer the Chamber of Horrors and models of pop idols *(see p66)*.

7 Fry Model Railway
A fascinating model railway museum with locomotives and coaches made by a retired railway engineer. ◈ *Malahide Castle, Malahide • Map N5 • Open Apr–Sep: daily; Oct: weekends only • Adm*

8 Kayaking
Children are attended by qualified instructors who take them kayaking in Dublin Bay. All equipment is supplied. ◈ *5 Tritonville Ave, Sandymount • Train Sandymount • Open summer only • Adm*

9 Lambert Puppet Theatre
Classic pantomime fun; performances range from fairy tales for toddlers to Yeats for older kids. ◈ *Clifton Lane, Monkstown • Train Salthill • 01-280 0974 • Open Sat–Sun*

10 Gotham Café
A fun fast-food outlet serving burgers and fries for hungry little visitors. ◈ *S Anne St • Map F5 • 01-679 5266 • Open noon–midnight Mon–Sat, 11:30am–10:30pm Sun • €*

Left **Royal Dublin Horse Show** Right **Six Nations Rugby**

🔟 Sporting Events

1 Royal Dublin Horse Show
Also known as the Kerrygold Horse Show, this is one of the world's top international equestrian events. Eleven competitions take place over the five-day event drawing more than 20,000 spectators. ⊗ *Merrion Rd • Train Sandymount • Early Aug*

2 Six Nations Rugby
The oldest stadium in the Six Nations Tournament holds 48,000 irrepressible Irish supporters during the nation's home games. ⊗ *62 Lansdowne Rd • Lansdowne station • Jan–Mar*

3 Leopardstown Christmas Racing Festival
Events occur year round at Leopardstown, but the four-day Christmas Racing Festival is one of the highlights of the Irish racing calendar. Built in 1888, the course offers some of the finest hospitality suites in racing. ⊗ *Leopardstown • 26–29 Dec*

4 Fairyhouse Racing Festival
Every Easter the historic Fairyhouse racing course hosts the Powers Gold Label Irish Grand National. ⊗ *Fairyhouse • Easter weekend*

5 Dublin City Marathon
Beginning on Aran Quay and winding through the city to finish back where it started, the Dublin Marathon attracts thousands of participants and spectators. ⊗ *Last Mon in Oct*

6 All-Ireland Hurling Final
Europe's oldest field sport uses a hockey-style stick partly to throw a ball down the pitch, but mostly to smack opposing players. The fastest field sport around, expect lots of excitement and a bit of blood. ⊗ *Croke Park • Train Heuston • Jul–Sep*

7 All-Ireland Football Final
Gaelic football is a mixture of soccer and rugby, though predating both games. The pace is similar to football, but allows the carrying of the ball, for a short distance, and adds goal posts to avoid those 0-0 draws. ⊗ *Croke Park • Train Heuston • Aug–Sep*

8 Laytown Races
The only horse race in the world run on a beach. As the tide rolls out, the finishing posts rise and bookies open shop. ⊗ *Laytown • Train Connolly • 10 Jun*

9 Dublin to Belfast Maracycle
Every year, in the middle of June, thousands of keen cyclists race each other from Dublin to Belfast, then back again.

10 Colours Boat Race
Crowds flock to the Liffey as Trinity and University College Dublin compete in the age-old rivalry of a rowing race between O'Connell Bridge and Sean Heuston Bridge, The tiny Ha'penny Bridge *(see p56)* fills with spectators. ⊗ *1 Apr*

Above **Details from a stained-glass window, depicting Irish legends**

Irish Legends and Myths

1 St Patrick
Patrick, a 5th-century Roman Briton, was captured by Irish raiders and taken into slavery in Ulster. Escaping to France, he became a priest and returned to Ireland to help convert the Irish. Extraordinary tales about him abound – he cured the sick, raised the dead, and rid Ireland of snakes by ringing his bell (see p30).

2 The Children of Lir
The greatest of the *Tuatha de Danann*, or fairy folk, was the sea-god Lir. His four beloved children were turned into swans by their jealous stepmother Aoife, who condemned them to live forever in the waters off the Ulster coast. Some 900 years later, St Patrick broke the spell, baptizing them as they died.

3 Punishment of the Children of Tuireann
For murdering his father, the sun god Lugh demanded that the three sons of Tuireann give him magical objects and perform difficult feats. Their last task was to make three shouts from the Hill of Miochaoin; these shouts summoned supernatural warriors who killed them.

4 Cuchulainn
The boy Setanta had miraculous strength and loved the game of hurling. Invited to a feast by the legendary black-smith Culain, Setanta arrived late and was met by the smith's ferocious guard dog. He killed the hound with his hurley stick and offered himself as a guard instead. He was renamed Cuchulainn, "hound of Culain".

5 Oisin in Tir na n'Og
Finn's son Oisin and Niamh, daughter of sea-god Manannan, went together to Tir na n'Og, paradise of eternal youth. After 300 years, homesick Oisin borrowed Niamh's magic horse to revisit Ireland. His feet were not to touch the ground, but he fell from the horse, instantly aged 300 years, and died.

6 Deirdre and the Exile of the Sons of Usnach
King Conchubar loved Deirdre, his harpist's beautiful daughter. The Druid Cathbad foretold she would bring disaster, so Conchubar kept her in solitude. But Deirdre loved young Naoise, son of Usnach,

Cuchulainn

who, with his brothers, took her to Scotland. After persuading them to return, Conchubar killed Usnach's sons. Deirdre, grief-stricken, killed herself.

7 Cattle Raid of Cooley
Connacht's Queen Medb (Maeve) raided Ulster to seize the chief Daire's famous bull. All the men of Ulster being under a spell, the boy Cuchulainn fought alone, killing all Medb's warriors. Medb retreated.

8 Pursuit of Diarmait and Grainne
Finn MacCoul asked King Cormac for the hand of his daughter Grainne, but she eloped with Finn's nephew Diarmait. For a year and a day Diarmait and Grainne fled as enraged Finn pursued them around Ireland.

9 Finn and the Salmon of Knowledge
The first person to taste the Salmon of Knowledge would gain prophetic powers. When the young Finn MacCoul – hero of countless legends – visited Finnegas, the old druid caught the fish. While it cooked, Finn's thumb touched the salmon. Putting the thumb to his lips, he tasted the fish before Finnegas.

10 Destruction of Dinn Rig
King Leary's brother Covac murdered Leary and his son at Dinn Rig, then forced the grandson to eat their hearts. Struck dumb until cured by Princess Moriatha's love, the grandson – renamed Labraidh ("Speaks") – grew up and reconquered Leary's kingdom. He then invited Covac to stay in an iron house on Dinn Rig. The door locked and a fire lit, all inside were roasted alive.

Top 10 Celtic Traditions

1 Celtic Crosses
High, richly carved stone crucifixes with a central circle are a feature of Celtic churches.

2 Celtic Design
Distinctive traditional interlocking patterns that decorate ancient Celtic jewellery have always remained popular in Ireland.

3 Language
The Irish language, spoken by about 1.5 million people today, comes directly from the ancient Celtic inhabitants.

4 Céilí
A get-together to drink, sing, dance and stamp your feet to traditional music.

5 Hurling
This robust Celtic game requires hurleys (ash sticks), a *sliotar* (a leather ball) and plenty of energy.

6 Musical Instruments
Uillean pipes, *bodhráns* (drums), tin whistles and other Celtic instruments remain at the heart of Irish folk music.

7 St Brigid's Crosses
Country people still weave rushes into these crosses and hang them up to protect against evil spirits.

8 Fairy Trees
An isolated tree in a field is generally not cut down because it is said to be sacred.

9 Water Worship
Sacred springs, fairy wells, and holy water remain a large part of many Irish people's religion.

10 Craic
The lively, witty, relaxed conviviality, gossip and talk that makes life worth living.

Left **Gaiety Theatre** Right **Gate Theatre**

🔟 Performing Arts Venues

1 National Concert Hall

For quality classical music, look no further: the National Concert Hall is Dublin's premier venue, hosting guests of the calibre of the New York Philharmonic. The building is also home to Ireland's National Symphony Orchestra. Jazz, contemporary and traditional Irish music are also performed here, and there are lunchtime concerts in summer. 🔍 Earlsford Terrace • Map F6 • Dis. access

2 The Abbey and Peacock Theatres

The Abbey is a legend. Founded in the early 20th century by a circle of writers including the poet WB Yeats, it gained renown at the cutting edge of Irish theatre. Controversial works by new writers such as Sean O'Casey and JM Synge were staged here, the latter causing riots on opening night. Now classics, these are the mainstay of the Abbey. Experimental work is shown in the sister theatre, the Peacock *(see p62)*.

3 The Gate Theatre

Since its founding in 1928, the Gate has been one of the most daring theatres in Europe, introducing Irish audiences to Ibsen and Chekhov and producing Oscar Wilde's *Salome* while it was banned in England. Orson Welles and James Mason both made their acting debuts here. Go early for a pre-performance drink in the cosy bar *(see p63)*.

4 The Gaiety Theatre

Dublin's oldest theatre dates from 1871. The gilded auditorium is an atmospheric backdrop for a wide range of entertainment, but, as its name suggests, the Gaiety leans more towards music and comedy. 🔍 S King St • Map E5 • Dis. access

5 The Olympia Theatre

Opened in 1879 as a music hall, after years of rivalry with the Gaiety the Olympia settled down to staging a similar gamut of musicals and comedy. 🔍 Dame St • Map E4

6 Andrew's Lane Theatre

This popular modern venue opened in 1989 in a converted warehouse. In its two intimate spaces touring companies perform drama and musical acts to a high standard. 🔍 9–11 Andrew's Lane • Map E5

Gaiety Theatre foyer

Olympia Theatre

7 Project Arts Centre
Born as a spin-off project to the Gate, the Project is perhaps the most vibrant centre of performance art in the city, with enthusiastic young companies exploring innovative dance, music, drama and poetry. U2, Liam Neeson and Gabriel Byrne were all rising stars here. ◈ *39 E Essex St • Map E3 • Dis. access*

8 Samuel Beckett Centre
The drama school of the university that produced Oscar Wilde and Samuel Beckett is set in a wonderfully intimate theatre space. Productions, often sparse in props, are rarely lacking in talent. ◈ *Trinity College • Map F4*

9 Tivoli Theatre
This 500-seat former cinema stages West End and Broadway musicals. The downstairs theatre doubles up as a rock venue at weekends. ◈ *135–8 Francis St • Map C5 • Dis. access*

10 Focus Theatre
Forget the mainstream: the emphasis here is on strong new US and European drama, which has earned it a place in Ireland's theatrical nobility. ◈ *6 Pembroke Place • Map H5 • Dis. access*

Top 10 Cultural Events

1 Dublin Theatre Festival
This two-week event showcases a wealth of Irish talent. ◈ *44 E Essex St • Map E3 • Late Sep–Oct*

2 St Patrick's Day Celebrations
A week-long series of events surrounds the parade on the day. ◈ *17 Mar*

3 Wexford Opera Festival
Performances of three different operas at Wexford's Theatre Royal, supported by daytime fairs. ◈ *Map P5 • Oct*

4 Galway International Arts Festival
Massive celebration of film, theatre, art, literature and music. ◈ *Map N2 • Jul–Aug*

5 Bloomsday
Fans of James Joyce re-enact his novel *Ulysses*, on the day it is set. ◈ *16 Jun*

6 Dublin International Film Festival (DIFF)
The best of Irish and worldwide cinema. ◈ *Spring*

7 Festival of Music in Great Irish Houses
Chamber music events in mansions near Dublin. ◈ *Jun*

8 Handel's Messiah
The Messiah has been sung every year since its first performance here in 1742. ◈ *St Patrick's Cathedral • Map D5 • Easter & Christmas*

9 Wicklow Gardens Festival
More than 40 private gardens open to the public. ◈ *May–Jul*

10 James Joyce Summer School
Seminars, tours and musical events. ◈ *Newman House, St Stephen's Green • Map E6*

Left **Mulligans** Right **The Long Hall**

TOP10 Pubs

1 Kehoe's

Just off Grafton Street, this cosy and recently refurbished pub has lost none of its original character. It's usually busy, but there's a large snug to hide away in, just beside the entrance. Close to Trinity College, it has a good mix of students and old pub characters. 🔊 *9 S Anne St • F5*

2 Ryans

This beautifully preserved pub has self-contained snugs – originally for "the ladies" – on each side of the counter. The decor is Victorian in every detail, from the mahogany partitions and sepia photographs to the brass match lighters fixed to the counter. Upstairs is a cosy restaurant which has won several awards. 🔊 *Parkgate St • Train Heuston*

3 Mulligan's

Once a working-class drinking man's pub (there were originally no chairs, since "real men" should stand as they drank), Mulligan's has since attracted a mixed bag, including former US President John F Kennedy. It is still stark, but cosy nonetheless, and constantly busy. For literature buffs, it features in the writings of James Joyce. Perhaps the best Guinness in Ireland: try a pint and cast your vote *(see p58).*

4 The Stag's Head

Built in 1770, the Stag's Head was refurbished in the opulent Victorian style, resembling a mix between a church and a mansion, with bottle-glass windows, mirrors reaching up to the high ceiling, a counter topped with Connemara marble, plus, of course, the scary antlered namesake on the wall. James Joyce also drank here, and it has featured in many films. A magnet for students, it tends to get lively. Good pub grub; but note it's closed on Sundays. 🔊 *1 Dame Court, off Dame St • Map E4*

Pub sign, **The Stag's Head**

5 Neary's

This cosy Edwardian-style pub, backing onto the Gaiety Theatre *(see p40),* is frequented by theatrical types, including, on occasion, Peter O'Toole. Writer Flann O'Brien used to have a tipple here too. 🔊 *1 Chatham St • Map E5*

The Long Hall
6 Backing onto Dublin Castle, this is very much a locals' pub, although many visitors come to experience its evocative atmosphere. The decor includes chandeliers and a pendulum clock more than 200 years old. ◈ 51 S Great George's St • Map D4

O'Donoghue's
7 Music and fun are the lifeblood of this pub, which fostered the popular balladiers, The Dubliners. Tap your feet on the Liscannor stone floor during an informal music session, or, if the sun's shining, have a drink in the little courtyard out back. ◈ 15 Merrion Row • Map F6 • Dis. access

Brazen Head
8 This pub, in the heart of Viking Dublin, is the oldest in the city. The building dates from the 1750s, but some believe there has been a tavern on this site since before the Norman invasion in 1172. The courtyard is a lovely spot for trying out one of the best pints of Guinness in Dublin and listening to traditional music. ◈ 20 Lower Bridge St • Map A3 • Dis. access

O'Donoghue's

Doheny and Nesbitt's
9 This building feels its age of 130 years, although Ned Doheny and Tom Nesbitt only set up the pub in the 1960s. Inside, a cosy snug and glass-panelled partitions create a perfect atmosphere for the lawyers, politicians and journalists who like to come here. ◈ 5 Lower Baggot St • Map G6

The Bailey
10 A watering hole and safehouse for Irish rebels such as Michael Collins, as well as literary figures such as Brendan Behan, the original building was demolished in the 1960s to make way for today's bright, airy bar. Dress is informal but stylish. ◈ 2–3 Duke St • Map F4 • Dis. access

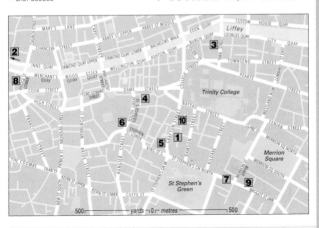

Left **Lillie's Bordello** Right **The International Bar**

Nightspots

1 The International Bar

You'd be content if this was just a watering hole – wood panelling and a healthy tradition make this one of the best drinking spots in town. Things get even better on music nights when bands play blues and soul upstairs. Tuesday is a singer-songwriter night and hosts some of Dublin's best talent. Comedy is on Thursdays *(see p58)*.

2 Break for the Border

If you tried to break for the border in this chain bar, you'd not get very far – on a Friday or Saturday night the crowds' gravity is sure to hold you in. Even in a club this size there are still queues and often standing room only. But then this is still a top spot and considered by many *the* place in town to be. ✎ *Johnson Place • Map E5*

Break for the Border

3 Club Anabel

This popular nightclub is located at the Burlington Hotel and attracts an older business crowd eager to unwind. The tourists from the Burlington add to the odd atmosphere, to make a club with many layers and cultures to appreciate. ✎ *Upper Leeson St • Map H5*

4 The PoD

A historic venue filled nightly with young Dubliners dressed to impress. "European Designer of the Year" Ron McCulloch planned the interior. The PoD's VIP bar is one of the city's most popular celebrity haunts. Features all-star DJs on a regular basis. ✎ *Old Harcourt St Station, Harcourt St • Map E6*

5 Lillie's Bordello

Not the place to chill out and have a pint of the black stuff, but nothing about Lillie's Bordello is traditional. You need to be a trend-setter to get through the door and celebrities frequent the private, reserved suites. Commoners compete to be seen and good music ties it together. ✎ *Adam Court, Grafton St • Map F4*

6 Temple Bar Music Centre

This venue attracts the best alternative rock bands and homegrown talent to its stage. Cutting-edge DJs fill the floors during the regular club nights and, once a week, the Centre hosts a salsa night (beginners welcome). ✎ *Curved St, Temple Bar • Map E4*

The Sugar Club

The Sugar Club
7 A relaxed candlelit venue where the crowd comes for the cocktail bar and performances – everything from casino nights and salsa to the "next big thing".
⊛ *8 Lower Leeson St • Map E5*

Club M
8 A Temple Bar institution, at the Blooms Hotel. There's a VIP lounge of some repute, great music and an interesting laser light system to add to the fun.
⊛ *Anglesea St • Map E4*

Rí-Rá
9 During the day, this bar is the smart, yet fashionable Globe, serving soups and sandwiches. Things change at 11pm. Rí-Rá opens as a thronging nightclub with a mixed gay/straight crowd.
⊛ *11 S Great George's St • Map E4*

Whelan's
10 It looks like your average pub, but walk through the bar to the back and you'll find one of Dublin's most happening venues.
⊛ *25 Wexford St • Map E6*

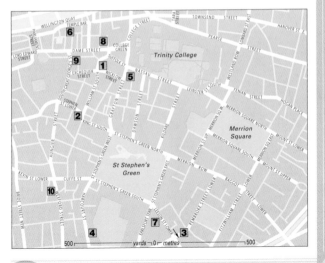

Left **Bewley's, Grafton Street** Right **Moore Street Market**

Shopping Areas

1 Grafton Street
Probably the most famous pedestrian thoroughfare in Dublin, Grafton Street traditionally caters to up-market shoppers, with homegrown department stores such as Brown Thomas *(see p57)*. Buskers offer a lively atmosphere. Bewley's, Dublin's famous tea house, has its most popular branch here *(see p53)*.

2 Powerscourt Townhouse
Irish designer labels and antiques shops cluster around the indoor courtyard of this 18th-century converted townhouse. Products range from handmade jigsaw puzzles to antique jewellery and Irish silver. The Design Centre is upstairs, with the cream of Irish fashion. When you've had enough, there are plenty of cafés here too *(see p55)*.

Grafton Street

3 Henry Street
Grafton Street's poor relation, Henry Street is lively and buzzing along its pedestrian route, while Moore Street's outdoor food market adds colour to the proceedings. Shops and department stores here tend to be better value than those south of the river. Arnotts department store is one of the most attractive in the city. ✪ *Map E2*

4 St Stephen's Green Shopping Centre
This delicate masterpiece of glass and light is a pleasant place to shop, filled with mainly chain stores such as Benetton and Tie Rack. On the top floor is the Dome restaurant, with great views of St Stephen's Green. ✪ *St Stephen's Green • Map F6 • Dis. access*

5 Francis Street
Dublin is one of Europe's best cities for antiques, and Francis Street and the surrounding area are an antique-hunter's dream, lined with deliciously dusty shops. Beware: the attitude may be relaxed, but the goods don't come cheap. ✪ *Map C4*

6 Jervis Street Shopping Centre
This large modern shopping centre contains shops selling food, household goods, fashion and sports gear. British chains such as Boots and Argos cater for most consumer needs. ✪ *1A Jervis St • Map E3 • Dis. access*

George's Street Arcade

7 Blackrock Market

A quick trip on the DART will take you out to the seaside village of Blackrock where, at weekends, an 18th-century tavern and courtyard house more than 60 stalls selling second-hand books, clothes and bric-à-brac, as well as genuine antiques. ✆ *Main St, Blackrock • Dis. access*

8 Liberty Market

Ideal for bargain-hunting, this market sells mainly fresh food and domestic goods. It's worth coming here just to soak up the atmosphere of one of the oldest areas of the city. ✆ *Meath & Thomas Sts • Map B4 • Thu–Sat*

9 George's Street Arcade

This lovely redbrick market has established shops on either side, with stalls down the centre. Exotic fruits rub shoulders with New Age baubles, fortune-tellers and vintage clothing. ✆ *S Great George's St • Map E5*

10 Westbury Mall

This covered walkway with boutiques and up-market cafés is a good place to escape a sudden downpour – all too common in Dublin. ✆ *Balfe St • Map E5*

Top 10 Food Sellers

1 Abbey Street Market

A mouthwatering display of international favourites, from Mexican *burritos* to Greek salads. ✆ *Map F2*

2 Temple Bar Market

The sale of farmhouse cheeses, organic vegetables and similar is soundtracked by street musicians. Weekends only. ✆ *Meeting House Sq • Map E3*

3 Moore Street Market

Last-chance bargains on vegetables, flowers and other produce. ✆ *Map E2*

4 Dunne & Crescenzi

Selling more than 100 Italian wines, fine olive oil and artisan products. ✆ *S Frederick St • Map F5*

5 Sheridans Cheesemongers

The best in Irish farmhouse cheese. ✆ *11 S Anne St • Map F5*

6 Thorntons Chocolates

Best choice of fine chocolates in Dublin from this well-known chocolate chain. ✆ *87 Grafton St • Map E5*

7 Bewley's

Bewley's are Ireland's finest tea shops, though the crowds often detract from the elegance. ✆ *11–12 Westmoreland St, Grafton St*

8 Berry Brothers

More than 800 fine wines to choose from here. ✆ *4 Harry St • Map E5*

9 Terroirs-Donnybrook

Fine wines and gourmet food sold in this elegant shop. ✆ *103 Morehampton Rd • Bus No. 10*

10 Avoca Food Hall

Foodstuffs from around the world and Irish crafts. ✆ *11–13 Suffolk St • Map D2*

Left **Patrick Guilbaud** Right **The Lobster Pot**

🔟 Restaurants

1 Patrick Guilbaud
Guilbaud's philosophy is "modern classic cuisine using Irish produce in season", but he does more than just dress up potatoes. He uses Ireland's bountiful fresh fish, meat and game to create savoury Gallic dishes. The restaurant is set in one of the brick townhouses that make up the Merrion Hotel *(see p128)*. Furnished in 18th-century style, it makes a great setting for this timeless cuisine. *◈ 21 Upper Merrion St • Map G5 • 676 4192 • Dis. access • €€€€€*

2 Rajdoot Tandoori
"Rajdoot" translates as "ambassador", and this multi-award-winning restaurant near Grafton Street has been a fine ambassador for tandoori cuisine since its establishment in 1966 as the first such restaurant in Europe. With chefs regularly sent back to India to train, the food is authentic north Indian, with a variety of inspired Moghlai presentations. *◈ 26–28 Clarendon St • Map E5 • 679 4280 • Closed Sun L • Dis. access • €€€*

Francesca's

3 La Stampa
A "modern Irish" restaurant with a Spanish name intrigues celebrities and local movers and shakers alike. The candlelit tables, modern art and mirrored dining room help too. The food, a combination of European dishes with a subtle dash of exotic Eastern flavours, keeps them coming back. Book ahead – the restaurant serves more than 1,800 meals a week and it may be difficult to get your hands on one. *◈ 35 Dawson St • Map E5 • 677 8611 • Dis. access • €€€€*

4 Roly's Bistro
Slightly out of the city centre, this lovely bistro serves dishes such as venison pie, in a relaxed and friendly atmosphere. *7 Ballsbridge Terrace • Train Lansdowne Road • 668 2611 • Dis. access • €€€€*

5 The Lobster Pot
A seafood restaurant set in a redbrick terrace house, the service and the cuisine are delightfully old-fashioned. As the name suggests, the chef uses as much fresh Irish sea catch as possible to produce favourites such as Kilmore crab and prawn bisque. *◈ 9 Ballsbridge Terrace • Train Lansdowne Road • 668 0025 • €€€*

6 Francesca's
A short walk from Temple Bar, Grafton Street and Dublin Castle, this sophisticated restaurant is part of the Brooks designer-boutique hotel *(see*

For a guide to price ranges **See p59**

La Stampa

p129). The food is a wonderfully creative take on traditional Irish ingredients, such as Dublin Bay prawns and wild Irish smoked salmon *(see p59).*

7 L'Ecrivain
Five minutes' walk from St Stephen's Green, this extremely popular award-winning restaurant creates original masterpieces from French-inspired dishes, accompanied by wines worthy of the food. Chef Derry Clarke and his team use fresh Irish ingredients to work the magic. Worth the price. Book ahead.
Ⓢ *190A Lower Baggot St • Map G6 • 661 1919 • Closed Sat L, Sun • Dis. access • €€€€€*

8 Tea Room at The Clarence
This beautiful hotel on the banks of the Liffey, owned by the rock band U2 is, not surprisingly, a celebrity and gossip-columnist magnet *(see p128).* If you come to celebrity-spot, you won't be disappointed by the food either, which is innovative in an interesting rather than pretentious way, as is

the ambience and the dramatic decor – the windows are two stories high. Winner of the Becks Taste of Temple Bar Award.
Ⓢ *Clarence Hotel, 6–8 Wellington Quay • Map D4 • 670 9000 • Closed Sat & Sun L • Dis. access • €€€€*

9 Mermaid Café
Within sight of Dublin Castle, this popular restaurant has all the elegance of an up-market establishment without any of the pretension. Simplicity is the keynote of the bright space and wooden decor, but not the cuisine. Enjoy the likes of confit of duck or pan-roasted Wicklow venison, or try a special from the chalkboard *(see p59).*

10 The Halo at the Morrison
This warm, atmospheric restaurant is in the chic new Morrison Hotel, on the north side of the Liffey *(see p128).* The trendy minimalist style and dramatic atrium setting is mirrored in the elegant Oriental fusion menu, which includes delicious coconut sauce dishes, seafood, and sauces as spicy as you dare. Dress is casual. Reservations recommended for dinner *(see p67).*

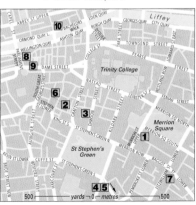

AROUND TOWN

DUBLIN'S TOP 10

Left **Trinity College** Right **St Patrick's Cathedral**

South of the Liffey

DUBLIN TAKES ITS NAME FROM THE SOUTHWEST OF THE CITY *when, in prehistoric times, there was a dark pool* (Dubb Linn) *at the confluence of the River Liffey and what was once the River Poddle. The area expanded during the 18th century, when the cobbled streets of Temple Bar became a centre for merchants and craftsmen – interestingly reverting to similar use in the 20th century. Prior to the founding of Trinity College in 1592, southeast Dublin was relatively undeveloped. St Stephen's Green wasn't enclosed until the 1660s and it remained for private use until 1877. But from the 1850s the area witnessed a boom that saw the construction of important public buildings such as City Hall. Today, the south is the hub of the fashionable scene, with designer stores and fine restaurants.*

🔟 Sights

1. Trinity College
2. National Museum
3. National Gallery
4. Dublin Castle
5. Temple Bar
6. Christ Church Cathedral
7. St Patrick's Cathedral
8. City Hall
9. Grafton Street
10. Powerscourt Townhouse

Christ Church Cathedral

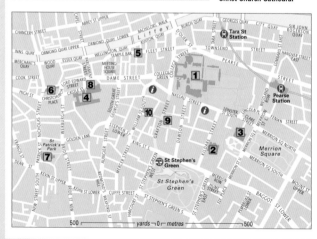

National Museum

Dublin Castle

4 Built into the city walls in 1204, the castle was Dublin's greatest stronghold, designed to defend the British-ruled city against the native Irish. It was at that time protected by rivers on both sides, the Liffey to the north and the Poddle to the south. The castle was completely reconstructed after a fire in 1684 and was further refined during the Georgian period, from which time most of the ornate state apartments date *(see pp14–17)*.

Temple Bar

5 This hugely popular area is the heart of south Dublin and has a seemingly limitless array of cafés, restaurants and bars as well as interesting little shops and cultural centres. On the banks of the Liffey, the term "bar" meant a riverside path. Its bustling atmosphere and trendy businesses, residents and clientele are the personification of Dublin's emergence in the 1990s as one of Europe's most fashionable and popular cities *(see pp18–19)*.

Trinity College

1 Ireland's premier institute of education was founded in 1592 by Queen Elizabeth I on the site of an Augustinian monastery. A Protestant-only college at its start, Trinity did open its doors to Catholic students in 1793, but it wasn't until the 1970s that the Catholic Church relaxed its opposition to the college. Its quadrangles are peaceful havens, and its priceless Book of Kells a highlight *(see pp8–9)*.

National Museum of Ireland

2 Only two of the museum's three sights are south of the river: the Natural History Museum *(see p56)* and the branch on Kildare Street which examines Irish archaeology and history. The latter's 19th-century building is almost as impressive as its collections, decorated with marble and mosaics *(see pp10–11)*.

National Gallery

3 A superb new wing of the gallery opened on Clare Street in January 2002, vastly increasing the space available for temporary exhibitions and displays of the gallery's permanent collection. The improved facilities also include a large shop, a café and restaurant and lecture theatres *(see pp12–13)*.

Temple Bar

City of Culture

Dublin's southside is the embodiment of the city's regeneration as a cultural hub for the Millennium. Numerous names associated with style and glamour have contributed to this trend: the Irish-born rock band U2 own one of the city's most stylish hotels, the Clarence *(see p128)* the internationally acclaimed fashion designer John Rocha works out of Dublin, and even the iconic songstress Marianne Faithfull has made the city her home.

6 Christ Church Cathedral

One of the city's two great cathedrals, illustrating the importance religion has always played in Dublin life, Christ Church was the first to be built, in 1038. Although nothing of the original wooden church now stands, there are plenty of beautiful medieval features and decorations to appreciate, including floor tiles and stone carvings. The "Treasures of Christ Church" exhibition, housed in the 12th-century crypt, includes a gilt plate donated by William III in 1697 *(see pp20–21)*.

7 St Patrick's Cathedral

Dublin's "second" cathedral and long-time rival to Christ Church. Apart from the many monuments and plaques com-memorating deceased dignitaries, and some fine architectural features, St Patrick's most interesting association is with Jonathan Swift. Appointed dean at the beginning of the 18th century, Swift carried out much of his work from the cathedral. You can see his death mask, writing desk and chair in the north pulpit and the memorial to himself and "Stella" lies just inside the entrance *(see pp22–3)*.

8 City Hall

Thomas Cooley built this stately building between 1769 and 1779. He had won the commission as a result of a competition, beating his better-known contemporary James Gandon who designed the Four Courts and Custom House *(see p56)*. Cooley made a fine job of City Hall, which was originally built as the city's Royal Exchange. City bureaucrats latterly used it for various purposes but, having undergone extensive restoration, it is now open to the public. There is an excellent permanent exhibition in the reconstructed vaults entitled "The Story of the Capital", covering 1,000 years of Dublin's fascinating history *(see p32)*.

⊗ Cork Hill • Map E4 • Open 10am–5:15pm Mon–Sat, 2–5pm Sun • Adm to exhibition

9 Grafton Street

Considered to be the premier shopping street on the south side of the Liffey, Grafton Street is also a pedestrianized venue for street musicians, performers and flower-sellers. There is the usual eclectic mix of high street shops, and ugly neon signs clash with the more

City Hall

Grafton Street

classical features of such shop-fronts as Marks & Spencer. The street runs south from College Green, marked by the statue of Molly Malone (irreverently known as "the tart with the cart"), opening out onto St Stephen's Green at the southern end. Brown Thomas (see p57) is one of the street's famous high-class department stores and Bewley's Oriental Café, with a shop at the front selling traditional Irish foodstuffs, is another popular landmark (see p59). ◎ Map E5

10 Powerscourt Townhouse

Built in the 18th century for Viscount Powerscourt, this fine building was converted into a shopping precinct in 1981. The main, grand entrance opens into a fine hall and staircase. The Georgian Room on the first floor, now turned into a shop similar to the other reception rooms, has exquisite plasterwork created by Michael Stapleton. There is a variety of stores here, including jewellery designers, trendy boutiques, craft outlets, coffee specialists and greengrocers. When you have exhausted your shopping cravings, there are plenty of places to eat and drink. ◎ S William St • Map E4

A Day Exploring the Southside

Morning

Breakfast in style at **Bewley's Oriental Café** (see p59) then spend the first half of the morning exploring the shops on **Grafton Street** and in **Powerscourt Townhouse** and soaking up the atmosphere of the street entertainers. Once the crowds move in, continue down to College Green and walk under the arch into **Trinity College** (see pp8–9) to relax in the grounds. On leaving Trinity, head down Dame Street to **Temple Bar** (see pp18–19) and enjoy the many shops and galleries here.

For lunch, press on to Leo Burdock's, the city's oldest fish-and-chip shop (2 Werburgh St • €). It's take-away only so make for **Christ Church Cathedral** (see pp20–21) and sit and admire its exterior while eating. Then wander inside to view the restored crypt and treasury.

Afternoon

After lunch, retrace your steps to **Dublin Castle** (see pp14–17) for a tour of the state apartments and a visit to the Chester Beatty Library. A cup of eastern-flavoured coffee and exotic cake in the café here will set you up for your final stretch of the day. Walk down Dame and Nassau streets to Clare Street and the newly opened Millennium Wing of the **National Gallery** (see pp12–13).

Finally, to unwind (albeit on rather a hard chair), check out an evening concert at **St Patrick's Cathedral** (see pp22–3).

Left & Centre **Government Buildings** Right **Merrion Square**

🔟 Best of the Rest

1 Dublinia
Entered via Christ Church Cathedral (see pp20–21), this exhibition uses audio-visuals to recreate medieval Dublin. ◈ St Michael's Hill • Map C4 • Open Apr–Sep: 10am–5pm daily; Oct–Mar: 11am–4pm Mon–Sat, 10am–4:30pm Sun • Adm

2 Ha'Penny Bridge
Built in 1816 to link the north and south sides of the Liffey, a halfpenny toll was once charged to cross it. ◈ Map E3

3 Government Buildings
Originally the Royal College of Science, these impressive buildings were quickly taken over by the government after independence in 1922. ◈ Upper Merrion St • Map G5 • Open Sat tours only • Adm

4 Mansion House
Designed in 1710 for aristocrat Joshua Dawson, this has been the residence of the city's Lord Mayor since 1715. ◈ Dawson St • Map F5 • Closed to the public

5 Bank of Ireland
Dublin's first Palladian-style building, built for the Irish Parliament in 1739, is beautifully floodlit at night. ◈ College Green • Map F4 • Open 10am–4pm Mon–Fri • Free

6 Natural History Museum
Stuffed animals and skeletons illustrate the natural world through the ages. ◈ Merrion St • Map G5 • Open 10am–5pm Tue–Sat, 2–5pm Sun • Free • Dis. access ground floor

7 Leinster House
This 18th-century home to the parliamentary chambers has two façades designed to reflect their views, the townhouse façade facing Kildare Street and the country house side looking on to Merrion Square. ◈ Kildare St • Map G5 • Open by appt only

8 Merrion Square
One of the largest and grandest of Dublin's Georgian squares, lined with stately buildings. Oscar Wilde (see p34) is one of many illustrious past residents of the square. ◈ Map G5

9 Iveagh Gardens
These little-known gardens are a lovely place to relax beside the rose bushes. ◈ Map E6

10 Shaw's Birthplace
The family home of playwright George Bernard Shaw (see p34), where he lived until the age of 20, gives a great insight into Victorian domestic life. ◈ 33 Synge St • Bus Nos. 16, 19, 122 • Open May–Sep: 10am–5pm Mon–Sat, 11am–5pm Sun; Closed 1–2pm • Adm

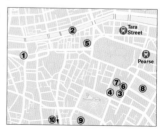

Left **Brown Thomas** Right **House of Ireland**

Top 10 Southside Shops

1 Brown Thomas
The smartest department store in town. A couple of floors of designer labels give the fashionistas plenty of scope, and there's also a great glass and china department featuring top Irish designs. ⊗ *Grafton St • Map E5*

2 Kilkenny Design
The best of Irish contemporary design for both men and women. Their own-label clothes are every bit as good as the designers they stock, and the prices are reasonable. Pottery, lights and glass objects are also on sale. ⊗ *5–6 Nassau St • Map E5*

3 Hodges Figgis
Ireland's answer to Waterstone's, a branch of which is opposite. Floors full of books covering all subjects and very good bargain offers available. Excellent children's section too. ⊗ *56–8 Dawson St • Map F5*

4 House of Ireland
Somewhat geared towards the tourist but nonetheless with an interesting range of Irish-made items, predominantly clothes, gifts and Waterford Crystal *(see p83)*. ⊗ *Nassau St • Map E5*

5 Whichcraft Gallery
Excellent gallery shop with highly original pieces of applied arts and crafts by over 350 Irish designers: from furniture and wall hangings to ceramics and jewellery. ⊗ *Cow's Lane • Map D4*

6 Celtic Note
This small shop specializes in Irish music records and CDs; it is difficult to pass by without being lured in by the Celtic tunes wafting into the street. ⊗ *12 Nassau St • Map E5*

7 Avoca Handweavers
For those who don't have a chance to visit Avoca in Powerscourt *(see p75)*, this shop is a satisfactory alternative, with its range of goods and clothes. Excellent food section, and a restaurant on the top floor. ⊗ *11–13 Suffolk St • Map E5*

8 JJ Fox Ltd
A Dublin institution, JJ Fox's cigarette and cigar emporium is definitely a place for connoisseurs. Specializes in Cuban and other fine cigars, and a wide range of smoking accessories. ⊗ *119 Grafton St • Map E5*

9 Kevin & Howlin
A traditional shop selling everything tweedy for men and women with conservative tastes, including the famous Donegal tweed. Wonderful old-fashioned service too. ⊗ *31 Nassau St • Map E5*

10 Celtic Whiskey Shop
This cosy shop offers a dazzling array of local Irish whiskeys in addition, of course, to the more famous brands. The service is as warm as a nip of the *uisce beatha* (water of life). ⊗ *28 Dawson St • Map F5*

For tips on shopping in Dublin **See p125**

Left **International Bar** Centre **O'Neills** Right **McDaids**

Pubs and Bars

1 The Porterhouse
Very popular with tourists and locals, who all come to sample the wide range of draught beers from this micro-brewery. It can become incredibly crowded so if you're dying of thirst this may not be the quickest place to quench it. ✆ 16 Parliament St • Map C4

2 The Odeon
A smart bar with plenty of space to sit, and the large windows onto the street make the place light and airy. The feel is sophisticated but the atmosphere remains relaxed. ✆ 57 Harcourt St • Map E6

3 International Bar
Popular with writers and musicians. The evenings of live music are exceptionally good (see p44) and well-attended. ✆ 23 Wicklow St • Map E4

4 Café en Seine
Recently reopened after a complete revamp, this is a trendy place in a central location. It attracts a regular young crowd keen on people-watching, as well as the after-workers. A good alternative to the traditional Dublin pub. ✆ 40 Dawson St • Map F5

5 McDaids
This pub offers literary tradition and an authentic old-style Dublin drinking experience, with stained-glass windows and old wooden interior. The writer Brendan Behan used to drink here so it's a stop-off for a popular Literary Pub Crawl. ✆ 3 Harry St • Map E5

6 Davy Byrne's
A friendly pub immortalized by James Joyce in his book Ulysses. Seafood and traditional Irish fare accompany the drink. ✆ 21 Duke St • Map F5

7 Oliver St John Gogarty's
This is both bar and restaurant, extremely popular with tourists for its central location in the middle of Temple Bar and more particularly for its traditional Irish food and music. ✆ 57 Fleet St • Map E4

8 Mulligans
Popular traditional old pub and a regular haunt of journalists and other print workers from nearby Fleet Street. Famous as the home of "the best Guinness in Dublin". ✆ 8 Poolbeg St • Map F3

9 O'Neills
The exterior of this pub is authentic and old-fashioned, while inside there are several different bar areas offering a variety of experiences and clientele. ✆ 2 Suffolk St • Map E4

10 SamSara
Chic and very laid-back looking bar with rattan chairs and natural fabrics. Plenty of space between tables too – rare in Dublin. ✆ Dawson St • Map E5

For Dublin's Top 10 Pubs See pp42–3

Above **Mermaid Café**

Price Categories

For a three-course meal for one with half a bottle of wine (or equivalent meal), taxes and extra charges.

€ under €25
€€ €25–€35
€€€ €35–€55
€€€€ €55–€70
€€€€€ over €70

🔟 Places to Eat

1 Jacob's Ladder
A very civilized place for lunch or dinner overlooking Trinity College *(see pp8–9)*. The food is a mixture of classic Irish and French. ✆ 4 Nassau St • Map F4 • 01-670 3865 • €€€€

2 MAO
In light, bright surroundings with minimalist decor, this informal Asian restaurant prides itself on efficient service and delicious food. ✆ 2–3 Chatham Row • Map E5 • 01-670 4899 • €€

3 Bewley's Oriental Café
Right in the centre of Grafton Street *(see p54)*, this is one of two branches of Bewley's in the city. The building alone is worth the visit, with stained-glass windows and authentic atmosphere. ✆ 78 Grafton St • Map E5 • 01-677 6761 • €

4 Botticelli
Genuine Italian run by Italians. The simple menu has all the old favourites – a good, reasonably priced place for lunch or dinner. ✆ 3 Temple Bar • Map E4 • 01-672 7289 • €€

5 Brownes Brasserie
The Brasserie is an informal name for the smart restaurant attached to this townhouse hotel. Right on St Stephen's Green and close to Grafton Street, it is convenient and the food excellent. ✆ 22 St Stephen's Green • Map F6 • 01-638 3939 • €€€€€

6 Francesca's
This hotel restaurant *(see p129)* specializes in modern Irish dishes. ✆ Brooks Hotel, 59–62 Drury St • Map E5 • 01-670 4000 • €€€

7 Dish
This small restaurant, with wooden floors and gilt-framed mirrors, serves Mediterranean dishes cooked to perfection. ✆ 146 Uppr Leeson St • Off map • 01-664 2135 • €€€

8 Pasta Fresca
Glass-fronted Italian with fresh pasta, pizzas and other dishes. ✆ 3 Chatham St • Map E5 • 01-679 2402 • €€€

9 Mermaid Café
A designer-style restaurant with contemporary furnishings and imaginative food. ✆ 69–70 Dame St • Map E4 • 01-670 8236. • €€€

10 Yamamori Noodles
Excellent Japanese cuisine. Soups, noodles and sushi in generous proportions. ✆ 71–72 S Great George's St • Map E4 • 01-475 5001 • €€

Around Town – South of the Liffey

 Note: *Unless otherwise stated, all restaurants accept credit cards and serve vegetarian meals*

Left **Mural, Abbey Theatre** Right **Custom House**

North of the Liffey

WHEN DUBLIN WAS DEVELOPED IN THE 18TH CENTURY, *plans for the north side of the River Liffey included a range of elegant terraces and squares designed to attract the city's élite. A downturn in the economy left the grand plan incomplete, although O'Connell Street and Parnell and Mountjoy Squares remain evidence of what might have been. The area boasts some of the city's most beautiful buildings, such as the Custom House and the Four Courts; three theatres, the Abbey, Peacock and the Gate, produce drama of worldwide acclaim; and the city's great literary tradition is celebrated in the Dublin Writers' Museum and James Joyce Cultural Centre. Although not as self-consciously stylish as the Southside, development plans are trying to rectify this with the revamp of areas such as Smithfield market (see p66).*

🗝️ Sights

1 Parnell Square
2 O'Connell Street
3 Custom House
4 Hugh Lane Municipal Gallery of Modern Art
5 James Joyce Cultural Centre
6 Dublin Writers' Museum
7 Abbey & Peacock Theatres
8 General Post Office
9 Old Jameson Distillery
10 Gate Theatre

Daniel O'Connell monument

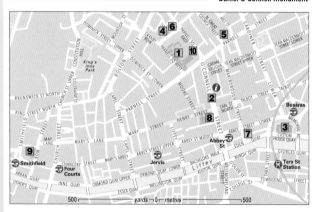

Parnell Square

1 The credit for this lovely Georgian square goes to Sir Benjamin Mosse, who founded the Rotunda Hospital here *(see p66)*. It was considered one of Dublin's smartest addresses in the 1760s, then its fortunes declined, but it remains home to some fine literary museums and art galleries. ◈ *Map E1*

O'Connell Street

2 One of the widest streets in Europe, O'Connell Street was designed by Luke Gardiner in the 1740s and was once lined with Classical buildings. Sadly, many of these were destroyed during the Easter Rising *(see p31)* and the street has lost the stately appearance of earlier times, but one of its remaining charms is its statues, the most imposing being that of Daniel O'Connell, near O'Connell Bridge. ◈ *Map E2*

Custom House

3 This magnificent building dominates the northside riverbank. Designed by James Gandon, the 114 m (375 ft) long façade is flanked by pavilioned arcades adorned with the Irish coats of arms. The 14 heads decorating the building represent

Custom House

Ireland's rivers. Restored in 1991, the building is now used as government offices. ◈ *Custom House Quay • Map G2 • Open mid-Mar–Oct: 10am–12:30pm Mon–Fri, 2–5pm Sat–Sun; Nov–mid-Mar: 10am–12:30pm Wed–Fri, 2–5pm Sun • Adm*

Hugh Lane Municipal Gallery of Modern Art

4 Art-lover Hugh Lane spent his life collecting important art, and today the permanent collection includes exceptional 20th-century work by Irish and European artists, including Manet and Degas. A new addition is the English painter Francis Bacon's London studio. ◈ *Charlemont House, Parnell Sq North • Map E1 • Open 9:30am– 6pm Tue–Thu, 9:30am–5pm Fri–Sat, 11am–5pm Sun • Adm for studio*

O'Connell Street

Nelson's Column

In the 1880s a controversial 50-m (164-ft) column topped with a statue of Nelson was erected in O'Connell Street. Several attempts were made over the years to destroy this symbol of British imperialism until, in 1966, a bomb damaged it so badly that it had to be dismantled.

5 James Joyce Cultural Centre

James Joyce *(see p34)* spent much of his early life living to the north of the Liffey so it is a fitting area to house a museum dedicated to the Irish writer. The house, built in 1784, was leased at the turn of the 20th century by Denis J Maginnis, who makes several appearances in Joyce's epic work *Ulysses*. There is a fascinating display of the biographical details of 50 of the 300 characters from *Ulysses* based on real Dubliners. ◈ *35 N Great George's St • Map F1 • Open 9:30am– 5pm Mon–Sat, 12:30–5pm Sun • Adm*

6 Dublin Writers' Museum

A mixture of faded parchments and a collection of portraits make up this original little museum. The Georgian proportions of the house are seen at

their best on the upper floors, with a grand Gallery of Writers. Downstairs, a taped commentary takes you through Irish literary history, accompanied by photographs, correspondence and first edition works. ◈ *18 Parnell Sq North • Map E1 • Open 10am– 5pm Mon–Sat, 11am–5pm Sun • Adm*

7 Abbey and Peacock Theatres

The Irish National Theatre was founded at the Abbey Theatre *(see p40)* by the Gaelic Revival Movement led by Lady Augusta Gregory and WB Yeats *(see p34)* and first opened its doors in 1904. From the outset it had a radical reputation, putting on revolutionary plays such as Sean O'Casey's *The Plough and the Stars*. The theatre then went into decline, before being gutted by fire in 1951. It reopened in 1966 as the Abbey and Peacock Theatres. The work performed at the Peacock is more experimental, while the Abbey stages conventional productions and new works. ◈ *26 Lower Abbey St • Map F2*

8 General Post Office

Designed in 1814 in Neo-Classical style by Francis Johnston, the GPO is one of the city's most imposing buildings. It was the centre of the aborted Easter Rising in 1916 and the scars of gunfire can still be seen on the Ionic portico. The history of this event can be seen in a sequence of paintings in the foyer by Irish artist Norman Teeling. ◈ *O'Connell St • Map E2 • Open 8am–8pm Mon–Sat • Dis. access • Free*

Dublin Writers' Museum

Chapter One Restaurant's theatre menu allows you to have a first and main course pre-performance and then return for dessert.

Old Jameson Distillery

A Day's Stroll Around the Northside

Morning

For an unusual breakfast head for the **Winding Stair Bookshop** (see p67) café, then browse its wonderful second-hand stock. Next, aim for **O'Connell Street** (see p61) and the **GPO**, where you can post your cards and view the historic bullet marks, and up to the **Gate Theatre** to book tickets for the evening's performance.

Be at the **Hugh Lane Municipal Gallery of Modern Art** (see p61) by 10am to have time to view the collection, then walk down to the **Dublin Writers' Museum**. Have lunch in the café before enjoying the literary artifacts. As you leave the museum, go downstairs to **Chapter One Restaurant** (see p67) and book a table for dinner.

Afternoon

After lunch, walk around the corner to the **James Joyce Cultural Centre**, then retrace your steps to the west side of **Parnell Square** (see p61) and the **Rotunda Hospital** (see p66) to have a look at the Baroque chapel.

For a bit of retail therapy, head for **Henry Street** (see p46), one of the city's main shopping areas. Continue down St Mary's Lane and up Bow Street to the **Old Jameson Distillery** for a tour and tot of whiskey.

Walk along the river past the floodlit **Custom House** (see p61) to enjoy a civilized pre-theatre drink at **The Gresham** hotel (see p129).

9 Old Jameson Distillery
The Old Jameson Distillery now exists purely as a museum, but whiskey was first made here in the 1780s and is as much a part of the Irish culture as Guinness (see pp24–5). The tour goes through the entire process of production, from grain delivery to bottling. At the end of the tour there is a whiskey tasting. The former distillery chimney is now a 67-m (220-ft) high observation platform with outstanding city views. ◈ Bow St • Map B3 • Open 9:30am–6pm daily • Dis. access • Adm

10 Gate Theatre
Originally known as The Assembly Rooms when completed in 1786, the building, designed by the German architect Richard Cassels, was converted into the Gate Theatre by the actors Hilton Edwards and Mícheál MacLiammóir in 1928. It soon established a reputation for high-class European productions, rivalling the Abbey, which concentrated on Irish plays. The Gate has maintained its standing as a venue for new plays but also puts on excellent productions of international and Irish classics. ◈ Cavendish Row, Parnell Sq East • Map E1 • Dis. access

 Following pages: Ha'Penny Bridge

Left **Baroque chapel, Rotunda Hospital** Right **Kings Inns**

🔟 Best of the Rest

1 Garden of Remembrance
Opened by Eamon de Valera in 1966 on the 50th anniversary of the Easter Rising *(see p31)*, this peaceful park commemorates all those who died in the fight for Irish Freedom. ⬡ *Parnell Sq • Map E1 • Open dawn–dusk • Free*

2 Rotunda Hospital
Designed by Richard Cassels, this was the first purpose-built maternity hospital in Europe when it opened in 1745. Inside is a beautiful Baroque chapel. ⬡ *Parnell Sq • Map E1*

3 St Mary's Pro Cathedral
Catholic Dublin has not had its own cathedral since the Reformation but St Mary's has been playing the part since 1825. It is home to the Palestrina choir, who sing the Sunday morning service. ⬡ *Marlborough St • Map F2 • Open 8:30am–6:30pm daily • Free*

4 Four Courts
This James Gandon master-piece is a majestic blend of Corinthian columns, copper lantern dome, arcades and arches. ⬡ *Inns Quay • Map C3 • Open 10am–5pm when court is sitting • Adm*

5 National Wax Museum
Geared more towards children than adults, with a Chamber of Horrors and a Wall of Mirrors as well as 300 wax exhibits *(see p36)*. ⬡ *Granby Row, Parnell Sq • Map D1 • Open 10am–5:30pm Mon–Sat, noon–5:30pm Sun • Adm*

6 Kings Inns
Designed by James Gandon in 1795 as a home for barristers. ⬡ *Henrietta St, Constitution Hill • Map C1 • Closed to the public*

7 Smithfield
This cobbled area, home to horse fairs on the first Sunday of the month, is also used for concerts. ⬡ *Map B3*

8 St Mary's Abbey
Founded in 1139. All that remains of the abbey is the vaulted chapterhouse. ⬡ *Meetinghouse Lane • Map D3 • Open mid-Jun–mid-Sep: 10am–5pm Wed & Sun • Free tours*

9 St Michan's Church
The attraction at this 11th-century church is the macabre mummified bodies. ⬡ *Church St • Map C3 • Open Apr–Oct: 10am–12:45pm, 2–4:45pm Mon–Fri, 10am–12:45pm Sat; Nov–Mar: 12:30–3:30pm Mon–Fri, 10am–12:45pm Sat • Adm*

10 GAA Museum
The Gaelic Athletic Association offers an insight into Irish sports. ⬡ *Croke Park • Drumcondra Station • Open 9:30am–5pm Mon–Sat, noon–5pm Sun • Adm*

Price Categories

For a three-course meal for one with half a bottle of wine (or equivalent meal), taxes and extra charges.

€	under €25
€€	€25–€35
€€€	€35–€55
€€€€	€55–€70
€€€€€	over €70

Left **Chief O'Neills** Right **Winding Stair Bookshop**

🄌 Places to Eat

1 Halo at The Morrison
Minimalist chic is the form here – the hotel *(see p128)* and restaurant were designed by the fashion supremo John Rocha. Modern European food with an Asian influence is put together with predominantly organic ingredients. ◈ *Ormond Quay • Map E3 • 01-887 2421• Dis. access • €€€€*

2 Chapter One
Warm colours, comfortable seating and courteous service set the tone. Excellent "theatre" dinner *(see p63)* and Irish and French cuisine. ◈ *18–19 Parnell Sq • Map E1 • 01-873 2266 • €€€€*

3 Chief O'Neills
This multilevelled open-plan eating and drinking place opens onto Smithfield's cobbled square. Good bar food. ◈ *Smithfield • Map B3 • 01-817 3838 • €€€*

4 101 Talbot Street
Just around the corner from the Abbey Theatre *(see p62)*. There's a choice of the main restaurant or the simpler Pasta Bar. ◈ *101–102 Talbot St • Map F2 • 01-874 5011 • €€*

5 Winding Stair Bookshop
The café of this great second-hand bookshop is an unpretentious place with some tables overlooking the Liffey. Wholesome soup, sandwiches, salads and cakes. ◈ *40 Lower Ormond Quay • Map E3 • 01-873 3292 • Closed D • €*

6 Clerys
The vaulted tearooms of this department store serve a lunch menu of salads, soup and sandwiches, but afternoon tea is their speciality. ◈ *O'Connell St • Map F2 • 01-878 6000 • Closed D • €*

7 Bangkok Café
No prizes for decor but the atmosphere is informal and the food always good. ◈ *106 Parnell St • Map F1 • 01-878 6618 • €*

8 Epicurean Food Hall
International food emporium with everything from kebabs to French cuisine. ◈ *Middle Abbey St • Map E3 • Open 9am–9pm • €*

9 Dublin Writers' Museum Café
At the back of the museum *(see p62)* this cheerful café has filling dishes as well as lighter snacks. ◈ *Parnell Sq • Map E1 • 01-873 2266 • Closed D • €*

10 Gresham Hotel
This grand hotel *(see p128)* offers a fine international menu, but head here for a particularly good afternoon tea. ◈ *O'Connell St • Map F2 • 01-874 6881 • Dis. access • €€€*

Note: Unless otherwise stated, all restaurants accept credit cards and serve vegetarian meals

Left **Phoenix Park** Centre **Powerscourt** Right **Kilmainham Gaol**

Greater Dublin

THE AREA AROUND DUBLIN'S CITY CENTRE IS RICH WITH ATTRACTIONS, *from stunning country estates – survivors of the Georgian heyday – to ancient Celtic remains and some spectacular scenery and walks, both in man-made landscaped surroundings or wilder natural settings. As in days gone by, many of Ireland's wealthy and well known choose to live in Dublin County's peaceful villages, benefiting from their close proximity to the capital while enjoying a more traditional way of life. The 10 sights selected here are less than an hour from Dublin as long as the journeys are undertaken outside the rush hours. A number of companies run day- or half-day trips to most of the sights within easy reach of Dublin.*

Russborough House

Sights

1. Guinness Storehouse
2. Kilmainham Gaol & Hospital
3. Phoenix Park
4. Powerscourt Estate
5. Castletown House
6. Russborough
7. Glendalough
8. National Stud
9. Newgrange & the Boyne Valley
10. Newbridge Demesne

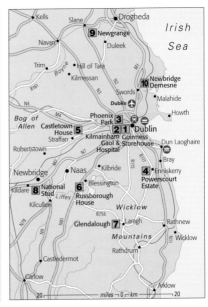

Guinness Storehouse

1 To the west of the centre, this comprehensive exhibition, set in the old brewery building, takes the visitor step-by-step through the creation of the famous beer, from the grain to the final glass of creamy topped black liquid *(see pp24–5)*.

Kilmainham Gaol and Hospital

2 At the far west of the city, these two institutions could not be more different. The forbidding Kilmainham Gaol, with its grim history, was restored and opened as a museum in the 1960s; in contrast, the former hospital is a fine and beautiful building, restored in the 1980s and now home to the Irish Museum of Modern Art *(see pp26–7)*.

Phoenix Park

3 There is enough to see within this vast park to keep the visitor busy for a whole day. The zoo is one of the main attractions and has recently claimed 33 acres out of the main park for its African Plains section for larger animals *(see pp28–9)*.

Powerscourt Estate

4 Five minutes from the pretty village of Enniskerry, Powerscourt Estate is a magnificent spot. The visitor approaches the house down a long beech-lined avenue with beautiful views across the valley. The house, designed by

Powerscourt

Castletown House

Richard Cassels in the 1730s, was gutted by fire in 1974, but a small exhibition gives the "before and after" story of its reconstruction. The main part of the house is now given over to an up-market shop *(see p73)* and large restaurant. The gardens are spread over a steep slope looking across to Sugar Loaf Mountain; steps lead down to a lake, where a Triton fountain hurls water high into the air. ◈ *Enniskerry, Co Wicklow • Map N5 • Open 9:30am–5:30pm daily • Dis. access • Adm*

Castletown House

5 This was the first example of Palladianism to be constructed in Ireland (1722–32) and remains the largest and most significant of its kind in the country. Architects Alessandro Galilei and Sir Edward Lovett Pearce built the house for William Conolly, the Speaker of the Irish Parliament. The fine interiors were commissioned in the second half of the 18th century by Lady Louisa Lennox, the wife of Conolly's great-nephew Tom, who took up residence here in 1758. The house remained in the family until 1965 and, after a period of ownership by the Georgian Society, is now run by the state. ◈ *Celbridge, Co Kildare • Map N5 • Open Apr–Oct: 10am–6pm Mon–Fri, 1–6pm Sat–Sun; Oct: 10am–5pm Mon–Fri, 2–5pm Sun; Nov–Mar: 2–5pm Sun • Dis. access • Adm*

Tour company buses to areas outside Dublin depart from the Central Bus Station, Busarus, in Store Street.

Gatehouses, Glendalough

6 Russborough

Another fine Palladian mansion, claiming the longest frontage in Ireland, Russborough was designed by Richard Cassels in the mid-18th century. Standing on raised ground it faces a stretch of water backed by the Wicklow Mountains (see pp80–81) and is kept in immaculate condition. One of the main reasons to visit is for the outstanding Beit Art Collection, put together in the 19th century by Sir Alfred Beit (1853–1906). His nephew bought Russborough in 1952 to house the collection. ◈ Blessington, Co Wicklow • Map N5 • Open May–Sep: 10am–5pm daily; Apr & Oct: 10am–5pm Sun & public hols only • Dis. access • Adm

7 Glendalough

A large part of the charm of this important monastic site is its location. The name translates as the "valley of the two lakes": the Upper Lake provides some of the most splendid scenery, with wooded slopes and a plunging waterfall, while the Lower Lake has a feeling of spirituality with the monastic ruins all around. St Kevin, a member of the Leinster royal family, founded the monastery during the 6th century and it became a renowned centre of Celtic learning. ◈ Co Wicklow • Map N5 • Open daily • Adm

8 National Stud

Visitors can tour this state-run bloodstock farm to learn about the breeding and training of these fine racehorses. The museum charts the development of the stud since its establishment by Colonel Hall Walker in 1900. Also within the estate are the beautiful Japanese Gardens, laid out between 1906–10 by Hall Walker and two Japanese gardeners to represent the "life of man". St Fiachra's Garden was created to mark the Millennium, named after a 6th-century monk with a love of gardening. ◈ Kildare • Map N5 • Open mid-Feb–mid-Nov: 9:30am–6pm daily • Dis. access • Adm

Upper Lake, Glendalough

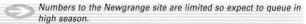

Numbers to the Newgrange site are limited so expect to queue in high season.

9 Newgrange and the Boyne Valley

Newgrange is one of the most significant passage graves in Europe but its origins are shrouded in mystery. Celtic legend tells that the Kings of Tara are buried here but Newgrange was certainly constructed earlier. All visitors must pass through the excellent Brú na Bóinne Visitor Centre and join a tour. Brú na Bóinne ("Palace of the Boyne") is the Irish name for the area, considered to be the origin of Irish civilization. Anyone with an interest in archaeology will find the Boyne Valley fascinating – its Hills of Tara and Slane also feature in Celtic mythology. ◈ Boyne Valley • Map M5 • Opening hours vary, but always open 9:30am–5pm daily • Adm

10 Newbridge Demesne

A must for architecture fans, this attractive house lies north of Dublin at the seaside village of Donabate. The house was designed for Archbishop Charles Cobbe in 1737 by George Semple – the Cobbe family still live in the upper half of the house although the council bought it from them in the 1980s. Rooms include the beautifully preserved Red Drawing Room, the huge kitchen and the Museum of Curiosities. ◈ Donabate • Map M5 • Open Apr–Sep: 10am–1pm, 2–5pm Tue–Sat, 2–6pm Sun; Oct–Mar: 2–5pm Sat–Sun • Adm

Newbridge Demesne

A Drive Around Greater Dublin

Morning

Head out of Dublin on the N4 west road to Celbridge and **Castletown House** (see p69). Take the first tour and you will get an excellent history of the house and family as well as being talked through the architectural highlights. Negotiate your way back to the Naas Road (N7) via Clane, across the Curragh towards Kildare and the **National Stud** – there's an excellent café here for a coffee. After a leisurely wander around the gardens, enjoy the fascinating and informative tour through the business of blood-stock.

After leaving here head for **Russborough House** by returning to Naas and taking the N81 Blessington road. The café-cum-restaurant at Russborough serves simple but delicious home-made fare for lunch. Then tour the house and savour the views of the **Wicklow Mountains** (see pp80–81).

Afternoon

Retrace your steps to Naas and the N7 to Dublin and follow signs for **Kilmainham Gaol** (see pp26–7). After a sombre visit to this former prison, cut across to **Kilmainham Hospital** for the Irish Museum of Modern Art. If further refreshment is required, there's a good café in the basement. Standing in the formal gardens here you get a great view across to **Phoenix Park** (see pp28–9) which you could visit on your way back into the centre, energy levels permitting.

Left **Malahide Castle** Centre **Howth** Right **Avondale House**

⏸ Best of the Rest

1 Glasnevin Botanic Gardens and Cemetery

These 47 acres include rose gardens and glasshouses. The adjacent cemetery is the final resting place of Daniel O'Connell (see p31). ⬡ Glasnevin Hill • Map N6 • Open 9am–6pm Mon–Sat, 11am–6pm Sun (summer); 10am–4:30pm Mon–Sat, 11am–4:30pm Sun (winter) • Dis. access • Free

2 Malahide Castle

The rounded towers of this 14th-century castle lend it an attractive fairytale appearance. ⬡ Malahide • Map N6 • Open daily • Adm

3 Howth

This busy fishing port offers great walks around the headland. Look out for seals when the boats come in. ⬡ Map N6

4 Sandycove Martello Tower

The first chapter of *Ulysses* (see p34) was set here and a tiny museum contains Joyce memorabilia. ⬡ Sandycove • Map N6 • Open Apr–Sep: 10am–5pm Mon–Sat, 11am–5pm Sun • Adm

5 Kilruddery House

Built in 1651 for the Earl of Meath, the formal gardens are its main feature. ⬡ Bray • Map N6 • Open Apr–Sep: 1–5pm daily • Adm

6 Mount Usher Gardens

A lure for all garden-lovers for its rare shrubs, flowers and trees. ⬡ Ashford • Map N6 • Open Mar–Oct: 10:30am–6pm daily • Adm

7 Avondale House

Charles Stewart Parnell (see p31) was born in Avondale House, which is now a museum dedicated to his memory. ⬡ Rathdrum, Co Wicklow • Map N6 • Open Mar–Apr, Sep–Oct: 11am–6pm Tue–Sun • Adm

8 Carlingford

This picturesque fishing village has a number of unusual buildings and a heritage centre. ⬡ Co Louth • Map N6

9 Peatland World

This exhibition on Irish bogs is in the heart of the Bog of Allen (see p98). ⬡ Rathangan • Map M5 • Open 9:30am–5:30pm Mon–Fri • Adm

10 Marino Casino

Built in the 1750s for the Earl of Charlemont, the casino was to serve as a summerhouse to his country estate. Restoration work is ongoing. ⬡ Fairview Park, off Malahide Rd • Map N6 • Open Jun–Sep: 10am–6pm daily; Oct & May: 10am–5pm daily; Nov–Dec, Feb–Mar: noon–4pm Sat–Sun; Apr: noon–5pm Sat–Sun • Adm

Left **Dalkey** Right **Avoca Handweavers**

Greater Dublin Shopping Areas

1 Powerscourt
Spread over two floors of the main house *(see p69)* are numerous different outlets. Avoca is the main retailer but there are plenty of others including Waterford Crystal and Powerscourt Own Brand. The garden centre is also excellent.
⊗ *Powerscourt House, Enniskerry • Map N6*

2 Fishers of Newtown Mount Kennedy
An unlikely place to find tucked away here, selling up-market women's fashions and traditional men's country clothes. ⊗ *The Old Schoolhouse, Newtown Mount Kennedy • Map N6*

3 Malahide
An extremely attractive village with its streets arranged in a cross-grid pattern. There is a variety of shops to visit including an excellent wine shop, designer boutiques and a well-stocked hardware store. ⊗ *Map N6*

4 Dalkey
Another pretty seaside village, and the home of many international stars. There is a couple of excellent galleries and designer boutiques selling pure linen clothes and original silk knitwear. ⊗ *Map N6*

5 Avoca Handweavers
This is one of the main outlets of Avoca, stocking a wide range of their own label clothes, gifts and foods. The self-serve restaurant sells huge helpings of Mediterranean food.
⊗ *Kilmacanogue, Co Wicklow • Map N6*

6 Mount Usher Gardens
This arcade of shops includes French label casual wear, equestrian clothes and equipment, a second-hand bookshop, art gallery and a pottery *(see p74)*.

7 Enniskerry
Yet another pretty Wicklow village with a smattering of designer shops: up-market gifts for the home in Enniskerry Trading Company, and great wine and cheese in Murtagh's Fine Foods and Wines. ⊗ *Map N6*

8 McGuirks
On the harbour in the centre of Howth *(see p74)*, this amazing shop sells excellent golfing gear at very keen prices as well as high-quality clothing that need not be confined to the golf course. ⊗ *Harbour Rd, Howth • Map N6*

9 Far Pavillion
The shop for a special gift. Pretty china, napkins and smelly things, as well as books, covered matchboxes and expensive salad bowls. ⊗ *16 Castle St, Bray • Map N6*

10 Wrights of Howth
Right on the pier, Wrights has a great selection of fresh fish – try the wild smoked salmon or gravadlax. ⊗ *14 West Pier, Howth • Map N6*

Around Town – Greater Dublin

Left **Johnnie Fox** Right **The Gravity Bar**

Pubs and Bars

1 Johnnie Fox
A well-known and respected pub, 3 miles (5 km) from Enniskerry. The 18th-century coaching inn, full of old beams and roaring open fires, has a seemingly endless series of connected rooms. Daniel O'Connell *(see p31)* was one of the pub's regulars and historic flyers decorate the walls.
◈ *Glencullen • Map N6*

2 The Gravity Bar
This is the highest point of the Guinness Storehouse and has stupendous views across the city. Enjoy your free pint – if you've been to the exhibition – and try to spot the various city landmarks from the panoramic windows *(see pp24–5)*.

3 The Roundwood Inn
Originally a 17th-century coaching inn, this relaxing place with wooden benches and floors is usually full of ramblers. The bar food is very good.
◈ *Roundwood, Co Wicklow • Map N6*

4 Lynhams Bar
A wonderful, welcoming pub with hearty fires and a jolly crowd of locals, just east of Glendalough. ◈ *Laragh, Co Wicklow • Map N6*

5 IMMA Café
A cheerful café in the basement of this art gallery, with painted tables and a light, bright atmosphere *(see pp26–7)* .

6 The Silken Thomas
This is both pub and restaurant and produces excellent and reasonably priced bar food. It is named after the fancy attire worn by a member of the Fitzgerald family in the mid-16th century, famous for rebelling against Queen Elizabeth I *(see p14)*. ◈ *Kildare • Map N5*

7 Polly Hops
A traditional old Irish pub with wooden and stone floors, good bar food and live traditional Irish music seven nights a week.
◈ *Lucan Rd, Newcastle, Co Dublin • Map N5*

8 PJ O'Hare Anchor Bar
A great institution, this old grocery store doubles up as a bar and is a fun place to drink. Oysters are a speciality when available. ◈ *Carlingford, Co Louth • Map M5*

9 Conyngham Arms
This old village inn is named after the family that own Slane Castle and most of the surrounding area. Originally a coaching inn, it is now also a hotel. Good food and a comfortable place to drink. ◈ *Slane, Co Meath • Map M5*

10 Abbey Tavern
There's a great atmosphere in this 16th-century inn, which makes the most of its antique features, large log fires and traditional Irish evenings. ◈ *Abbey St, Howth • Map N6*

Price Categories

For a three-course meal for one with half a bottle of wine (or equivalent meal), taxes and extra charges.	€ under €25
	€€ €25–€35
	€€€ €35–€55
	€€€€ €55–€70
	€€€€€ over €70

Above **King Sitric**

🔟 Places to Eat

1 King Sitric
Right at the end of Howth's harbourfront is this respected restaurant. The freshest seafood is on offer in comfortable surroundings. Good views from the first floor. Reservations essential. ◈ *East Pier, Howth • Map N6 • 832 5235 • Dis. access • €€€€*

2 Avoca Café Powerscourt
A simply decorated café serving the Avoca kitchens' well-tested fare. Spread over a number of large rooms, the acoustics can be a bit wearing when it's full. Wonderful views from the terrace *(see p69)*.

3 Hungry Monk
A slightly quirky but high-quality restaurant, specializing in game and fish. A new wine bar on the ground floor is an excellent addition to the village. ◈ *Church Rd, Greystones • Map N6 • 287 5759 • €€€*

4 Oscar Taylor's
Situated on the Portmarnock coast road, this restaurant offers good food, and fabulous views of Lambay Island and the Malahide Estuary. ◈ *Island View Hotel, Coast Rd, Malahide • Map N6 • 845 0099 • €€–€€€*

5 Poppies
Cheap and cheerful cottage-style restaurant that looks and feels like an English tearoom. Generous portions of reliable home cooking. ◈ *The Square, Enniskerry • Map N6 • 282 8869 • €*

6 Brasserie Na Mara
A very special restaurant in what used to be the Customs Hall. Lots of space and light with high ceilings and attractive decor. The seafood menu is delicious. ◈ *The Harbour, Dun Laoghaire • Map N6 • 280 6767 • Dis. access • €€€*

7 Café Mao's
The same idea as the original restaurant in Chatham Row *(see p59)*; the space here is bigger and airier – very much suited to the style of the food. ◈ *The Harbour, Dun Laoghaire • Map N6 • 214 8090 • Dis. access • €€*

8 Cavistons
This small, smart restaurant has a reputation for producing mouth-watering fish dishes. It is only open for lunch but has three sittings, so the last can run into an early supper. ◈ *59 Glasthule Rd, Sandycove • Map N6 • 280 9245 • €€€*

9 40 Foot
Named after the traditional bathing area on Sandycove shore, this trendy bar-restaurant has magnificent views of Dublin Bay. Up-to-the-minute style and delicious food. ◈ *The Pavilion, Dun Laoghaire • Map N6 • 284 2982 • €€*

10 Kish
This purpose-built restaurant beside an apartment development is elegant but informal and the food is outstanding. Good-value lunch menu. ◈ *Coliemore Rd, Dalkey • Map N6 • 285 0377 • €€€€*

> **Note:** Unless otherwise stated, all restaurants accept credit cards and serve vegetarian meals

AROUND
IRELAND

DUBLIN'S TOP 10

Left **Sally Gap** Right **Wicklow Gap**

TOP 10 **Wicklow Mountains**

1 Sally Gap
This bleak and remote crossroads on the mountain road between Dublin and Glendalough stands at one of the highest mountain passes in Ireland. With its extensive areas of watery bog, the country is so inaccessible around here that it was a favourite hideout for Irish warriors and nationalist rebels during the centuries of conflicts between the English and Irish forces. ❂ Map N5

2 Wicklow Gap
This high point on the little R756 road through the Wicklow Mountains is also on the mountain route to Glendalough from Dublin. Turn here to climb up to the 2,670-ft (816-m) Tonelagee viewpoint, with its breathtaking panoramic view. There are few places that better capture the lonely beauty of this mountain range. ❂ Map N5

Rural cottage, Wicklow Mountains

3 Wicklow Way
For those who really want to see the mountains at close hand, there's nothing better than walking. Numerous easy marked local paths run through pretty hill country, while the Wicklow Way is for serious hikers. This 82-mile (130-km) marked path makes its way through the heart of the region, all the way from Dublin to Clonegal, in County Carlow. ❂ Map N5

4 Blessington and The Lakes
The delightful Georgian village of Blessington is where the beautifully preserved Palladian mansion Russborough House, and its famous Beit Art Collection, is to be found. From here, yet again, there are good views of the mountains while, just south of the village, the River Liffey has been dammed to form a picturesque lake reservoir, popular with Dubliners for picnic outings and water-sports. ❂ Map N5

5 Wicklow Town
Wicklow's modest county town has a low-key charm, with its harbour and unpretentious pubs. The one unmissable sight is Wicklow Gaol. A shocking tale is told at this notorious historic jailhouse (closed in 1924), where hundreds of Irish rebels were detained, often tortured and, in many cases, hanged. Evocative exhibitions fill in the background, including a section on the

deportation of the inmates to the colonies, such as Australia. ◈ *Map N6 • Wicklow Gaol: Open mid-Apr–Sep: 10am–6pm daily; Adm*

6 Djouce Woods

Close to Dublin, this steeply hilly woodland is part of the Powerscourt Estate. With the beautiful Powerscourt Waterfall at its centre, it is a popular area for an outing from the city, especially for walks, picnics, jogging and orienteering. Deer and red squirrel can be seen among the oak, Sitka spruce, Douglas fir, beech and chestnut trees. ◈ *Map N5*

7 Avondale Forest Park

The beautiful Avondale Forest Park is filled with marked walks and nature trails, some of them along the bucolic setting of the River Avonmore banks. There is also an 18th-century arboretum within the park, with an impressive range of plant species. ◈ *Rathdrum • Map N5 • Open daily • Adm*

8 Vale of Avoca

"There is not in the wide world a valley so sweet," wrote 19th-century poet Thomas Moore in his work *The Meeting of the Waters*. It is perhaps not as idyllic now as it was then, but the meeting of rust-coloured rivers among wooded hills is still enticing. Avoca Handweavers, at the nearby village *(see p75)*, produce wonderful authentic tweeds in Ireland's oldest handweaving mill. ◈ *Map N5*

9 Devil's Glen

Although close to Wicklow Town, this romantic wooded glen, with its waterfall and chirruping birds, is a haven of peace and tranquillity. It is part of the pretty valley of the Vartry. Perfect for walking or riding, it makes a quiet escape within an hour's drive of Dublin. There are many pleasant self-catering apartments and cottages to rent, as well as stables, and other holiday facilities. ◈ *Map N5*

10 Clara Lara Fun Park

A top recreation site for families, the fun park is in the Vale of Clara, and near the village of Laragh – hence the name. Its rides are mostly based around water, but there are Go Karts, too, and the highest slide in Ireland, as well as tree-houses, climbing frames and picnic areas. ◈ *Map N5*

View of the Wicklow Mountains

Left **Hook Peninsula** Right **Stone carving, Jerpoint Abbey**

Around Waterford

GREEN AND HILLY COUNTY WATERFORD *is exposed to the Atlantic to the south, the beautiful Blackwater and Suir rivers penetrate far inland, while Waterford City stands by an excellent natural harbour. All these factors made this corner of the southeast almost too welcoming to outsiders – Waterford City (Vadrafjord in Norse), founded in AD 853, is thought to be the oldest surviving Viking town in Europe. Later, Normans also chose this spot for their first Irish settlement – in few other places can Celtic, Norse and Norman relics be found so close to one another. In modern times, Waterford has been staunchly patriotic and proud of its heritage – it even has a small Gaeltacht (Irish-speaking district) around the village of Rinn.*

🔟 Sights

1. Waterford Crystal Factory
2. Waterford Treasures at the Granary Museum
3. Waterford City Centre
4. Ardmore
5. Jerpoint Abbey
6. Hook Peninsula
7. Passage East
8. Reginald's Tower
9. Dunmore East
10. John F Kennedy Park and Arboretum

Reginald's Tower

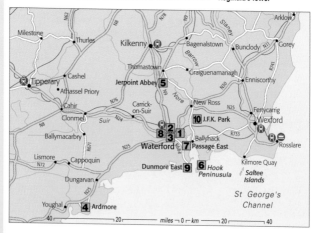

Waterford Crystal Factory

1 Waterford Crystal Factory

Most visitors to Waterford come specifically to see its famous glassworks – and buy whatever they can afford of its renowned "crystal". First opened in 1783, closed in 1851 and reopened in 1947, the factory has always used the same production methods, every item being individually hand-crafted. A 40-minute tour and a film show off the astonishing skill of the glassblowers and cutters, while the Crystal Gallery displays an array of what is made. *Cork Rd, Waterford • Map Q5 • Open Mar–Oct: 9am–4:15pm daily; Nov–Feb: 9am–3:15pm Mon–Fri • Dis. access • Adm for tour*

2 Waterford Treasures at the Granary Museum

This old stone grainstore has been cleverly and attractively converted to house an extraordinary interactive museum revealing Waterford's impressive Viking and Norman history. It gets in the mood with an invader's-eye view from a wave-tossed Viking ship. Kids love it, and there's a lot that is just for fun, but the more serious-minded can ignore the wizardry and focus on the archaeological finds. *Waterford • Map P5 • Open daily • Dis. access • Adm*

3 Waterford City Centre

Surviving sections of Waterford's city walls show clearly the limits of the original Viking settlement, also bordered on one side by the River Suir. Today that waterfront, with its lively and attractive quays, is the focal point of the town. The 18th-century City Hall houses important local memorabilia, and hosts the Waterford Show, an entertainment about the town's history. *Map P5*

4 Ardmore

Modern Ardmore is a popular little beach resort, but the hill behind is the site of St Declan's 5th-century monastery, probably the oldest in Ireland. Its many evocative remains (mostly dating from the 12th century) include St Declan's Cathedral, a fine example of a high cross, and an impressive, 30-m (100-ft) round tower. *Map Q4*

5 Jerpoint Abbey

One of Ireland's best examples of a Cistercian monastery, the restored chapterhouse and part of the cloisters of 12th-century Jerpoint stand grandly among its ruins in a peaceful countryside setting. The Jerpoint community quickly established itself as a great centre of culture and learning, and was very prosperous at the time of the Dissolution in 1540. Many fine pieces of stone-carving can be seen, and there is a useful Interpretative Centre. *Thomastown • Map P5 • Open Mar–Nov: daily; Dec–Feb: open for bookings only • Dis. access • Adm*

Hook Peninsula

6 Hook Peninsula
The peaceful "Ring of Hook" headland lies beside the broad Waterford Harbour, with long sandy beaches, rugged cliffs, and many relics of the past. At the northeast corner, ruined Tintern Abbey – with beautiful grounds and a little stone bridge – was founded in 1200 and, although much altered, remains atmospheric. The peninsula's wild tip, where there has been a lighthouse since the 5th century, is beloved of bird-watchers. ◈ Map Q5 • Tintern Abbey: Open Jun-Oct: 9:30am–6:30pm daily; Dis. access; Adm

7 Passage East
A small, enjoyable ferry runs to-and-fro across Waterford Harbour from this unassuming waterside village. Its peaceful, scenic setting and handful of painted cottages make a pleasant break while waiting for the boat. It was at this spot that the Normans arrived in Ireland in 1170 and their sturdy stone tower still stands guard over the harbour. ◈ Map Q5

8 Reginald's Tower
The circular stone fortification built 1,000 years ago by Ragnvald, son of Sygtrygg, was part of the original Viking ramparts and still dominates the quayside. Over the centuries it provided a base for other invaders, including Strongbow, Henry II, King John and Richard II, as well as doing time as a prison. Today it houses an art gallery and a museum of Waterford history.
◈ Quay, Waterford • Map P4 • Open Jan–Oct: daily; Nov–Dec: Wed–Sat • Adm

9 Dunmore East
A working fishing harbour with brightly coloured boats, and cottages set among woods, this attractive village makes a favourite outing for a drink, lunch or a waterfront stroll. Many of the cottages are available for holiday lets. Nearby sandy coves include the popular Lady's Cove beach, and there are several enjoyable marked walks and hikes. ◈ Map Q5

10 John F Kennedy Park and Arboretum
Some 4,500 international species of trees and shrubs – all carefully labelled – grow in this delightful 600-acre arboretum, created in memory of the former US president. Just below the arboretum stands the humble thatched cottage where the president's great-grandfather was born.
◈ New Ross • Map P5 • Open daily
• Dis. access • Adm

Waterford's Gaeltacht

The only Irish-speaking area in the southeast is in County Waterford. The village and peninsula of Rinn, on the south side of Dungarvon Harbour, is known as the *Deisi Gaeltacht* after the Deisi tribe whose home this was. A Gaelic College here offers further education in the language.

Price Categories

For a three-course meal for one with half a bottle of wine (or equivalent meal), taxes and extra charges.

€	under €25
€€	€25–€35
€€€	€35–€55
€€€€	€55–€70
€€€€€	over €70

Above **Dunbrody Country House**

🔟 Places to Eat

1 Lady Helen Dining Room
One of the region's more sophisticated restaurants serves an imaginative menu with international influences. The restaurant has two AA rosettes. ⌾ *Mount Juliet, Thomastown • Map P5 • 056 777 3000 • Dis. access • €€€€*

2 Bianconi
This award-winning hotel restaurant serves the best of contemporary, Italian-influenced cuisine and has an excellent wine list. ⌾ *Granville Hotel, Waterford • Map P5 • 051 305555 • Dis. access • €€€*

3 Ocean Hotel
This excellent restaurant has won awards for its menu, which is strong on freshly caught local seafood. ⌾ *Dunmore East • Map Q5 • 051 383136 • €€*

4 Rinuccini
Serving an appetizing blend of classic Italian dishes and the best of modern Irish cooking (with the emphasis on seafood, game, and Irish beef and lamb). ⌾ *1 The Parade, Kilkenny • Map P4 • 056 776 1575 • €€€*

5 Dunbrody Country House
Owner Kevin Dundon is regarded as one of Ireland's finest cooks, and the restaurant of this fine country house hotel is elegant, with outstanding food and an excellent wine list. ⌾ *Arthurstown • Map P5 • 051 389600 • Dis. access • €€€€*

6 The Olde Stand
This centrally located pub-restaurant (which has twice been given the Irish Pub of Distinction award) has a friendly atmosphere and serves excellent steak and seafood. ⌾ *45 Michael St, Waterford • Map P5 • 051 879488 • Dis. access • €€*

7 The Cellar
Chef Billy Whitty has received international acclaim for his modern take on traditional Irish farmhouse cooking, with dishes such as marinated venison. ⌾ *Horetown House, Foulksmills • Map P5 • 051 565771 • Dis. access • €€€*

8 The Lobster Pot
This cheerful pub-restaurant near the sea (prettily decorated with hanging baskets) serves fine seafood at a price that won't break your budget. ⌾ *Carnsore Point, Carne • Map P5 • 053 31110 • Dis. access (partial) • €€€*

9 The Sky and the Ground
Quirky pub restaurant with a fine choice of classic dishes and almost 300 wines from its own wine shop, at off-licence prices. ⌾ *112 S Main St, Wexford • Map P5 • 053 21273 • €€€*

10 Loughman's
A good choice for those on a budget, this friendly café has a wide choice of vegetarian dishes and Irish and European favourites. ⌾ *George's Court, Barrowstand St, Waterford • Map P5 • 051 878704 • Closed D • Dis. access • €*

Note: Unless otherwise stated, all restaurants accept credit cards and serve vegetarian meals

Left **Lacemaking, Kenmare** Right **Caha Mountain, Beara Peninsula**

The Ring of Kerry and the Dingle Peninsula

THE SOUTHWEST OF IRELAND IS ONE OF THE MOST BEAUTIFUL *regions* of the country. The Killarney National Park is an experience in itself but, if at all possible, like the Ring of Kerry, should be seen off-season – the area has become so popular that driving the Ring can turn into a nightmare of tour buses in high season. The area is largely made up of peninsulas, among them three to the southwest of Kenmare, the stunning Dingle Peninsula to the north, and the most popular, the Beara Peninsula, with two impressive mountain ranges running along its spine, offering wonderfully dramatic views. Yet, it's not all nature. Amid this landscape, both peaceful and rugged in turns, are some striking Georgian residences, numerous pretty villages, wildlife reserves and ancient religious sites. A journey to this corner of the country will have something to suit all tastes and expectations.

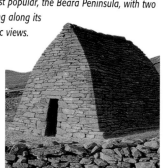

Gallarus Oratory

🔟 Sights

1. Lakes of Killarney
2. Beara Peninsula
3. Dingle
4. Kenmare
5. Bantry Bay & Bantry House
6. Gallarus Oratory
7. Killarney
8. Derrynane House
9. Sneem
10. Valentia Island and the Skelligs

1 Lakes of Killarney
The three lakes in this region, Upper, Middle (Muckross) and Lower (Lough Leane), are linked by the Long Range River and are all incorporated into the stunning 100-sq km (40-sq mile) Killarney National Park. Flanked by mountains, and with a varied landscape of woodland, heather and peat bogs, the area offers a range of beautiful walks and drives.
⊗ *Killarney, Co Kerry • Map Q2*

2 Beara Peninsula
The largest of the western peninsulas has something for everyone, with its pretty villages, beaches and mountains. The two ranges here are the Slieve Miskish and Caha Mountains. Tortuous bends wend their way to the summits, but it's worth it for the view on fine days. If you are interested in wildlife, take the cable car across to Dursey Island, with its sea bird colonies.
⊗ *Co Cork and Co Kerry • Map Q1*

3 Dingle
A small, attractive fishing town with a fine natural harbour, Dingle is extremely popular with tourists, who appreciate its charm. Fungi the dolphin is the town's most famous resident and people come for miles to see him play. ⊗ *Co Kerry • Map Q1*

Dingle harbour

4 Kenmare
Designed by the Marquess of Lansdowne in 1775, this prosperous town has more of a continental atmosphere here than Irish, with its smart shops and fine restaurants. Kenmare's greatest claim to fame, however, is more traditional, as a centre of lacemaking. ⊗ *Co Kerry • Map Q2*

5 Bantry Bay and Bantry House
This market town and fishing port is named after its beautiful situation at the head of Bantry Bay. Bantry House, commanding an outstanding position with views across the bay, has been owned by the White family since 1739. For maritime enthusiasts there is a small museum in the stable, examining the history of the French Armada, which was scuttled here in 1796. ⊗ *Bantry, Co Cork • Map Q2 • Bantry House: Open mid-Mar–Oct: 10am–6pm daily, Adm*

Upper Lake, Killarney

The Skelligs

The history of the Skellig Islands dates back to the 7th century when St Finian founded the monastery of Skellig Michael. All that remains now are the ruins of the church, two oratories and six beehive cells perched on a narrow platform. From 1820 to as recently as 1987, the lighthouses here were looked after by solitary lighthousekeepers. Skellig Michael was designated a World Heritage Site in 1996.

6 Gallarus Oratory

The best preserved early Christian site in Ireland is believed to have been built some time between the 6th and 9th centuries AD. It was exquisitely constructed, using Neolithic techniques, with fine dry-stone corbelling to ensure the structure was waterproof. ⬡ *Smerwick, Co Kerry • Map Q1*

7 Killarney

On the doorstep of the Ring of Kerry, with a clutch of excellent hotels and old-fashioned ponies and traps, it's not surprising that this attractive town becomes inundated with visitors in summer. The shops and restaurants are worth the visit, let alone the surrounding scenery. ⬡ *Co Kerry • Map Q2*

Killarney

Sneem

8 Derrynane House

Derrynane is a lovely spot on the coast, with 3 km (2 miles) of dunes and beaches. Derrynane House was the family home of Catholic politician and lawyer Daniel O'Connell *(see p31)* and it now contains a museum dedicated to the great leader. ⬡ *Co Kerry • Map Q1 • Open Apr & Oct: 1–4:15pm Tue–Sun; May–Sep: 9am–5:15pm Mon–Sat, 11am–6:15pm Sun; Nov–Mar: 1–5pm Sat–Sun • Adm*

9 Sneem

This pretty village, backed by the 682-m (2,240-ft) Knockmoyle Mountain, resembles something out of a children's picture book, with its houses all painted different colours. A popular, friendly place. ⬡ *Co Kerry • Map Q2*

10 Valentia Island and the Skelligs

The Skellig Experience museum, near the causeway linking Valentia Island to the mainland, includes exhibits on the history of the Skellig Michael monastic site and a range of information on local flora and fauna. Valentia is a popular holiday spot and is particularly good for watersports, but the only inhabitants of the Skelligs now are the birds. Cruises circle the islands but do not land. ⬡ *Co Kerry • Map Q1*

Above **Bantry House café**

Price Categories

For a three-course meal for one with half a bottle of wine (or equivalent meal), taxes and extra charges.

€ under €25
€€ €25–€35
€€€ €35–€55
€€€€ €55–€70
€€€€€ over €70

Places to Eat

1 Packies
The hallmark of Maura Foley's cooking is simplicity and purity of ingredients. Relaxed and informal setting. ⬤ *Henry St, Kenmare • Map Q2 • 064 41508 • Closed Sun, Nov–Easter • €€*

2 Sheen Falls
Everything about the Sheen Fall Lodge is grand. The hotel is immaculately run, exuding sophisticated style. The restaurant is no exception and the food is faultless. ⬤ *Kenmare, Co Kerry • Map Q2 • 064 41600 • Dis. access • €€€€€*

3 Annie's Restaurant
Chef-owner Annie Barry uses fresh local produce to create Irish dishes with a European twist. Set in a pretty seaside village, it is very popular, so book ahead. ⬤ *Ballydehob, West Cork • Map Q2 • 028 37292 • Closed Sun–Mon, Nov • Dis. access • €€€*

4 Doyle's Seafood Bar
In an area awash with seafood, this relaxed restaurant serves traditional fish dishes alongside more adventurous concoctions. ⬤ *Dingle, Co Kerry • Map Q1 • 066 915 1174 • €€€*

5 The Purple Heather
Simple food but cooked to perfection – pâtés to die for, beautifully light omelettes and hearty sandwiches on home-made bread. ⬤ *Kenmare, Co Kerry • Map Q2 • 064 41016 • €–€€*

6 Nick's Restaurant
This is an extremely relaxed and jolly place very popular with the locals, with generous portions of traditional dishes. ⬤ *Lower Bridge St, Killorglin, Co Kerry • Map Q2 • 066 976 1219 • Dis. access • €€€*

7 Gaby's
Run by the Maes family who have been in the business for decades, Gaby's is considered to be one of the best fish restaurants in town. ⬤ *17 High St, Killarney, Co Kerry • Map Q2 • 064 32519 • Dis. access • €€€*

8 Bantry House
This fine house *(see p87)* overlooking Bantry Bay has a craft shop and an excellent café with informal seating. ⬤ *Bantry, Co Cork • Map Q2 • 027 51796 • €*

9 The Cooperage
Modern in style and decor, this bar and restaurant attracts a younger crowd than many of the other local restaurants in this price range. ⬤ *Old Market Lane, Killarney, Co Kerry • Map Q2 • 064 37716 • Closed Sun L • Dis. access • €€€*

10 Chart House Restaurant
This informal modern restaurant is to the east of town with windows overlooking the harbour. The food combines many flavours, with both Asian and European influences. ⬤ *The Mall, Dingle, Co Kerry • Map Q1 • 066 915 2255 • Closed Tue • Dis. access • €€€*

Note: *Unless otherwise stated, all restaurants accept credit cards and serve vegetarian meals*

Left **Barley Cove, Cork** Right **Cobh**

Around Cork

CORK CITY AND THE SURROUNDING AREA *are full of historic, cultural and scenic places to visit. Cork itself is a lovely city, worth one or two days' exploration, including the three islands in Cork harbour formed by the two sections of the River Lee. Cobh, situated on what is known as Great Island, came into its own in the 19th century as an important naval base, due to its huge natural harbour. Close by is Fota Wildlife Park and Arboretum, offering the visitor a change of pace from the predominance of water and sea. Between Cork and Youghal, the small town of Midleton*

boasts the oldest distillery in Ireland, Jamesons, home to the famous Irish whiskey. The equally well known Blarney Castle, with its "magic" stone, is only a short trip to the north of Cork. To the south, Kinsale is a charming fishing village full of places to eat and its fair share of comfortable accommodation, making it a good base for exploring the area.

Blarney Castle

🔟 Sights

1. Cork City
2. Kinsale
3. Cobh
4. Youghal
5. Blarney Castle
6. Fota Wildlife Park & Arboretum
7. Timoleague Abbey
8. Jameson Heritage Centre
9. Charles Fort
10. Royal Gunpowder Mills

Cork City

1 Officially Ireland's second city, built on either side of the River Lee, Cork is a true rival to Dublin according to the local residents, of which there are around 140,000. The picturesque quays both north and south of the river, linked by an array of bridges, offer spectacular views. The numerous waterways, narrow alleys and Georgian buildings, together with the balmy climate, often lend the city a more continental than Irish atmosphere. ◉ *Map Q3*

Kinsale

2 The fact that Kinsale has its own gourmet food festival gives some idea of the calibre of restaurants and cafés here. It is probably the most prosperous and sophisticated fishing village in the country and, being only 15 km (9 miles) from Cork, attracts locals and tourists in droves. The pretty harbour is the focal point and most of the activity centres on this area and the backstreets around it. ◉ *Map Q3*

Cobh

3 Pronounced "Cove", this 19th-century town boasts one of the world's largest natural harbours. In its heyday, the town was a major commercial seaport as well as being the stop-over port for luxury passenger liners,

Kinsale

Youghal

including the *Sirius*, which made her maiden voyage from here. Cobh was also the last port of call for the *Titanic* before she sailed to her tragic end. The Queenstown Story is an interesting exhibition detailing the town's maritime history. Particularly poignant is the section on the part Cobh played in the transportation of convicts to Australia in the 18th and 19th centuries. ◉ *Map Q3*
• *The Queenstown Story: Cobh Heritage Centre, Open daily, Dis. access, Adm*

Youghal

4 About 30 km (18 miles) east of Cork, Youghal (pronounced "Yawl") has a great location on both the Atlantic Ocean and the tamer banks of the River Blackwater's estuary. The impressive walls enclosing the town are evidence of its vulnerability to attack from France and Spain – it was once one of the most heavily fortified seaports on the British coast. Queen Elizabeth I bestowed Youghal on Sir Walter Raleigh in gratitude for faithful service. Under Cromwell, however, the town became an English Protestant garrison. ◉ *Map Q4*

5 Blarney Castle
It is really the Blarney Stone, believed to have been brought to Ireland during the Crusades, that brings visitors flocking here in their masses. Legend has it that whoever kisses the stone will be given the gift of eloquent speech. The castle itself dates from the mid-15th century and the Banqueting Hall and Great Hall are fine examples of architecture of the period. ◌ *Blarney • Map Q3 • Open daily • Dis. access • Adm*

6 Fota Wildlife Park and Arboretum
This 700-acre centre prides itself on helping to protect the environment, breeding and reintroducing animals to their natural habitats. One of its great successes is the saving of the native white-tailed eagle that was threatened with extinction in Ireland. ◌ *Carrigtuohill, Cobh • Map Q3 • Open Apr–Oct: daily • Dis. access • Adm*

Blarney Stone, Blarney Castle

Old Midleton Distillery

7 Timoleague Abbey
A bleak atmosphere presides here, when the mist hangs over the shore and the ruined 13th-century Franciscan abbey sits broodingly on the waterside. Of particular interest is the wine cellar – the friars prospered on the importation of Spanish wines in the 16th century. ◌ *Timoleague • Map R3 • Open daily • Free*

8 Old Midleton Distillery
An excellent audio-visual presentation of the story of Irish whiskey, with a tour of the still houses, granaries, mills and maltings, and a highly popular whiskey tasting. ◌ *Midleton • Map Q3 • Open daily • Adm*

9 Charles Fort
Built in the late 17th century, Charles Fort has been associated with some of the most momentous events in Irish history, including the Williamite War of 1690 and the Irish Civil War in 1922–23. ◌ *Summer Cove, Kinsale • Map Q3 • Open daily • Adm*

10 Royal Gunpowder Mills
Gunpowder was one of Cork's most important industries in the mid-19th century until the mills closed in 1903. Visitors can see the canals, sluices, weirs, mills and workers' cottages. ◌ *Ballincollig • Map Q3 • Open mid-Apr–Oct: daily • Dis. access • Adm*

Price Categories

For a three-course meal for one with half a bottle of wine (or equivalent meal), taxes and extra charges.

€ under €25
€€ €25–€35
€€€ €35–€55
€€€€ €55–€70
€€€€€ over €70

Above **The 1601**

TOP 10 Places to Eat and Drink

1 Aherne's Seafood Restaurant and Bar

This popular, relaxed restaurant, serving delicious fresh seafood dishes, brings people from miles around. 🌐 N Main St, Youghal • Map Q4 • 024 92424 • Dis. access • €€

2 The Yumi Yuki Club

Cork's first sushi bar opened in 2001 and is a huge success. The chef's selection, served on unmatching plates, sets the tone and livens the tastebuds. 🌐 Triskel Arts Centre, Tobin St, Cork • Map Q3 • 021 427 5777 • €€

3 Blair's Inn

This award-winning bar-restaurant is full of nooks and crannies, with open fires in winter and a beer garden in summer. The speciality is seafood: try the lemon sole stuffed with crab meat. 🌐 Cloghroe, Blarney, Co Cork • Map Q3 • 021 438 1470 • €€€

4 The Vintage

On the market side of town, this bar and restaurant is housed in an ancient beamed building, with natural stone walls and tiled floors. The food is wholesome and well cooked. 🌐 O'Brien St, Kanturk • Map Q3 • 029 50549 • Closed Sun L • €€€

5 Isaacs

Very popular with locals and visitors the simple, unpretentious food is consistently good. 🌐 48 MacCurtain St, Cork • Map Q3 • 021 450 3805 • Closed Sun L • €€

6 Ballymaloe House

Darina and Tim Allen's cookery school held here has a worldwide reputation and it is hardly surprising that the food is absolutely delicious. Booking is essential. 🌐 Shanagarry • Map Q3 • 021 465 2531 • Dis. access • €€€€

7 The 1601

This pubs serves a straightforward menu of good bar food in modern surroundings. 🌐 Pearse St, Kinsale • Map Q3 • 021 477 2529 • €

8 An Súgan

An extremely popular pub with seafood dishes to absolutely die for. 🌐 41 Wolfetone St, Clonakilty • Map Q3 • 023 33498 • Dis. access • €€€

9 Crackpots

Eating here is an interesting experience because you are surrounded by unusual artwork and pottery – hence the name. The food is an equally unusual mix of styles and flavours and the atmosphere is relaxed and informal. 🌐 3 Cork St, Kinsale • Map Q3 • 021 477 2847 • €€

10 Kinsale Gourmet Store and Seafood Bar

Looking at the quality and the choice of fresh fish on sale at the fishmongers inspires one to try the excellent food served at the simple, informal seafood bar. 🌐 Guardswell, Kinsale • Map Q3 • 021 477 4453 • Closed D • €€€

Left **Rock of Cashel** Right **Limerick**

Tipperary, Limerick and Clare

FROM THE LUSH GREENERY OF TIPPERARY to the traffic jams of Limerick, and from the leisurely vacation boats cruising on the wide river Shannon up to the stark, stirring emptiness of The Burren, this region embraces the full diversity of rural Ireland. There are scores of impressive historic sights and picture-perfect villages, as well as unpretentious country towns with not a tourist in sight. Cross the Shannon to reach the rockier majesty of County Clare, whose rural way of life retains a profound simplicity and sense of independence. Culturally, it is rooted in tradition, and you'll hear plenty of Irish music played in village pubs. Clare's coastline rises in dramatic cliffs that take the force of the Atlantic, while inland, wind-battered gorse and bracken are broken up by high pasture. Sheep wander unfenced, walking over the hills and along the country lanes as if all this land was theirs.

Cliffs of Moher

Sights

1. Cashel
2. Limerick
3. Cliffs of Moher
4. The Burren
5. River Shannon
6. Kilrush and Loop Head Drive
7. Bunratty Castle
8. Foynes Flying Boat Museum
9. Ennis
10. Killaloe

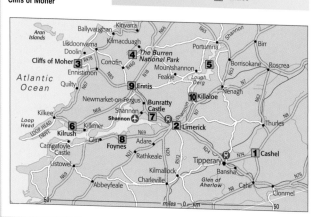

1 Cashel

This quiet country town is dominated by the awesome Rock of Cashel, topped by stone structures known in pre-Christian times as Cashel of Kings (from Gaelic *caiseal*, a stone fortress). Sensing the rising power of the church, in 1101 the Kings of Munster redefined themselves as a dynasty of royal archbishops and built great ecclesiastical buildings. Most were destroyed by the English in 1647, but highlights of what survives are 12th-century Cormac's Chapel, the earliest Romanesque church in Ireland; the roofless 13th-century cathedral; and the 15th-century Vicars' Choral, the residential quarters of the cathedral cantors. *Cashel • Map N2*

2 Limerick

A grim portrait of industrial Limerick, the third-largest city in the republic, was painted by Frank McCourt's novel *Angela's Ashes (see p35)*. It's not that bad now. The city centre has good restaurants and pubs and a pleasant atmosphere. Historical sights include the imposing King John's Castle, built in 1210, containing a display on the town's 800-year history. Don't miss, either, the Hunt Museum, a magnificent collection of Irish antiquities inside the beautiful 18th-century Old Custom House. *Map P3 • King John's Castle: Open daily; Adm • Hunt Museum: Rutland St; Open daily; Adm*

3 Cliffs of Moher

Five miles (8 km) of sheer cliffs rising as much as 650 ft (200 m) up from the pounding Atlantic, this is one of Europe's grandest stretches of coastline. Take the cliff-edge footpath round to O'Brien's Tower, which gives a stunning view. *Map N2*

4 The Burren

A weird limestone desert of flat rock "pavements", at first glance most of the 100-sq-mile (260-sq-km) Burren (pronounced "burn") seems lifeless. But the web of hidden gulleys is brimming with plants, some very rare. Once densely populated, the Burren preserves dolmens, ruined towers and ring-forts. Visit the Display Centre to learn more. *Map N2 • Burren Display Centre: Kilfenora; Open daily, Adm*

The Burren

5 River Shannon

Ireland's longest river opens into broad lakes, eventually widening into a huge estuary. The river's curve traditionally marks the border of the west. Lough Derg, the largest lake, set amid wooded hills, is a popular area for boating and angling. Further downriver is an immense variety of birdlife. ⊗ *Map P2*

6 Kilrush and Loop Head Drive

While Kilrush itself is unremarkable, it makes a good base for exploring the furthest reaches of southwest County Clare. Especially worthwhile is a drive out to remote Loop Head. For an insight into local history, particularly the hardships of the region under English rule, visit the Kilrush Heritage Centre. ⊗ *Map P2 • Kilrush Heritage Centre, Market House: Open May–Sep: 10am–5pm Mon–Sat; Adm*

7 Bunratty Castle

The sturdy 15th-century stronghold of the O'Briens, Earls of Thomond, has become the top venue for mock medieval banquets and other entertainment. The five-storey structure was fully restored by Viscount Gort in

Banqueting room, Bunratty Castle

Burren Botany

Apart from seasonal pools, called *turloughs*, the Burren's limestone does not hold water. Yet more than 1,000 plant species thrive here, because countless cracks in the rocks and stones accumulate organic matter and provide shelter. Especially common are mosses, lichens, rock rose, mountain avens, orchids and bloody cranesbill.

1954. Behind the castle, Bunratty Folk Park gives insight into traditional rural culture. ⊗ *Bunratty • Map P3 • Open 9:30am–5:30pm daily; Last adm to castle 4pm • Adm*

8 Foynes Flying Boat Museum

Transatlantic flights between Ireland and the US began in Foynes in 1939, and in 1942 the first non-stop passenger flights between America and Europe started here. The museum tells the story. There is also a 1940s-style tearoom. ⊗ *Foynes • Map P2 • Open Apr–Oct: 10am–6pm daily • Adm*

9 Ennis

This likeable little town, with its bright shopfronts and music pubs, first grew up in the 13th century around the Franciscan community of Ennis Friary. Shut down in 1692, the abbey fell into ruin but what survives – mostly 15th-century – includes the richly carved MacMahon Tomb. ⊗ *Map P2 • Friary: Open mid-May–Sep: 9:30am–6:30pm daily; Dis. access; Adm*

10 Killaloe

A chic marina town rising steeply from the southern end of Lough Derg, Killaloe is a centre for watersports. Its 12th-century St Flannan's Cathedral and Oratory have Romanesque decorative stonework. ⊗ *Map P3*

Price Categories

For a three-course meal for one with half a bottle of wine (or equivalent meal), taxes and extra charges.

€	under €25
€€	€25–€35
€€€	€35–€55
€€€€	€55–€70
€€€€€	over €70

Above **The Mustard Seed**

Places to Eat

1 Brulees
Donal Cooper and Teresa Murphy serve fine food made mainly from local produce at their widely acclaimed restaurant in central Limerick. ❧ *Henry St, Limerick • Map P3 • 061 319931 • Dis. access • €€€*

2 Durty Nelly's Oyster Restaurant
This mellow village inn, in the shadow of Bunratty Castle, has been in business since 1620, and still serves a range of substantial Irish dishes, oysters and seafood. ❧ *Bunratty • Map P3 • 061 364861 • Dis. access • €€€*

3 Earl of Thomond
This aristocratic room at Dromoland Castle is the perfect place for a lavish lunch or dinner after a day on the adjoining golf course. ❧ *Newmarket on Fergus • Map P3 • 061 369144 • €€€€€*

4 The Seafarer
This long-established local in the centre of Lahinch village (handily near the golf club) is renowned for fine poultry, seafood, beef and lamb. ❧ *Kettle St, Ennistymon Rd, Lahinch • Map P3 • 065 708 1050 • Dis. access • €€€*

5 Molly's Bar and Restaurant
A pub-style restaurant on the shores of Lough Derg, Molly's serves simply cooked, fresh local produce. ❧ *Balina, Killaloe • Map P3 • 061 376632 • Dis. access • €€*

6 Hal Pino's
This stylish new bar-restaurant, just off Ennis's main square, serves an eclectic menu drawing on worldwide influences in an up-scale but informal atmosphere. ❧ *7 High St, Ennis • Map P3 • 065 684 0011 • Dis. access • €€€*

7 Cruises
Established in 1647, Cruises is an attractive, old-style inn with superb steak and seafood and live traditional music every night. ❧ *Abbey St, Ennis • Map P3 • 065 684 1800 • Dis. access • €€€*

8 The Mustard Seed
This bustling restaurant within a Victorian country house hotel offers fine modern Irish cuisine and an excellent wine list. Stylish, but not pretentious. ❧ *Echo Lodge, Ballingarry • Map P3 • 069 68508 • Dis. access • €€€€*

9 The Arches
This is an affordable, family-run eatery in the centre of one of Ireland's prettiest villages and is well known for its hearty home cooking and friendly service. ❧ *Adare • Map P3 • 061 396246 • No credit cards • Dis. access • €€*

10 Cullinans
This family-owned restaurant (and guesthouse) in the centre of Doolin village is renowned for its speciality of locally caught fresh seafood, simply prepared and presented. ❧ *Doolin • Map P3 • 065 707 4183 • Dis. access • €€€*

Note: Unless otherwise stated, all restaurants accept credit cards and serve vegetarian meals

Left **Clonmacnoise ruins** Right **Shannonbridge Bog Railway**

🔟 Around Clonmacnoise

1 Clonmacnoise

This early Christian site, founded by St Ciaran in the 6th century, draws tourists into Ireland's often neglected Midlands. The grounds are atmospheric, especially on a grey Irish day, and include the ruins of a cathedral, eight churches (10th–13th-centuries), two round towers, three high crosses and dozens of early Christian grave slabs. The visitors' centre offers an audio-visual show and exhibitions. ✆ *Shannonbridge • Map N4 • Open Mar–May & Sep–Oct: 10am–6pm daily; May-Sep: 9am–7pm daily; Oct–Mar: 10am–5:30pm daily • Dis. access (visitors' centre) • Adm*

2 Birr Castle, Gardens and Telescope

It's rare that a castle plays second fiddle to its surroundings. Here, however, the gardens, covering more than 150 acres and containing 2,000 species of rare trees and shrubs, take the prize. Spring blossoms and autumn foliage are mesmerizing. The grounds are also home to the Earl of Rosse's 72-inch (180-cm) telescope. Built in the 1840s this was once the world's largest. ✆ *Rosse Row, Birr • Map N4 • Open daily • Dis. access • Adm*

3 Emo Court

Designed in 1790 for the Earl of Portarlington, this is another fine example of architect James Gandon's work *(see p53)*, and his interiors in this lovely

Emo Court

house remain unchanged. The fine gardens are divided into two sections: the Grapery leads you down to a lakeside walk; the Cluckery acquired its name from the nuns who used to reside here. ✆ *Portlaoise • Map N4 • House: Open mid-Jun–mid-Sep: 10:30am–5pm Tue–Sun; Gardens: Open dawn–dusk daily • Adm to house*

4 Shannonbridge Bog Railway

You might call it dirt, but they call it peat around these parts, and it is valuable. Bord na Mona (the national peat board) runs this 5.5-mile (9-km) rail trip through the Blackwater Bog and the Blackwater Power Station. The tour teaches you everything you need to know about harvesting this acidic resource and the importance it has played in powering the Emerald Isle. ✆ *R357, Shannonbridge • Map N4 • Open Apr–Oct • Adm*

5 Birr

Although largely dominated by the castle and its grounds, the town of Birr has much to offer visitors. Its beautiful

Georgian style has been lovingly preserved, many of the buildings retaining their original fanlights and door panelling. ⊗ *Map N4*

6 Rock of Dunamase

Towering 150 ft (45 m) above a flat plain, the Rock of Dunamase is one of the most impressive and historic sights in Ireland. The sight was included on Ptolemy's world map in AD 140, such was its fame, and the ruins date back thousands of years. Standing amid its history, you can see all the way to the Slieve Bloom Mountains. ⊗ *Laois • Map N4*

7 Belvedere House

Despite a perfect Austen-style setting, there was no sense or sensibility in the actions of the Earl of Belvedere. He began the house in 1740, spent his life fighting his brothers and built the Gothic Jealous Wall to block the view of his sibling's house. He also imprisoned his wife for 31 years, suspecting she'd slept with one of them. Visitors, however, are free to roam the beautiful gardens and the shore of Lough Ennell. ⊗ *N52, Mullingar • Map N4 • Open May–Aug: 9:30am–6pm Mon–Fri, 10:30am–7pm weekends; Sep–Oct: 10:30am–6pm daily; Nov–Apr: 10:30am–4:30pm daily • Dis. access • Adm*

8 Tullynally Castle

Originally constructed in the 17th century, most of Tullynally today is a result of the second Earl of Longford's remodelling of it as a rambling Gothic Revival castle, housing a collection of Irish furniture and portraits. Outside are romantic grounds and walled gardens. ⊗ *Castlepollard • Map M4 • Castle: Open to groups by arrangement; Gardens: Open May: weekends, Jun–Aug: 2–6pm daily • Adm*

9 Slieve Bloom Mountains

Despite only rising 2,000 ft (615 m), the surrounding flat plain aids in creating an imposing image of the Slieve Bloom Mountains. The summits have been declared a National Nature Reserve and the Slieve Bloom Way has been marked out for hikers who have waterfalls, hidden glens and peaceful villages to look forward to. ⊗ *Map N4*

10 Bog of Allen

Once the largest raised peat bog in Ireland, the bog has been gradually shrinking as it is used for powering the island. It is home to some of Ireland's most interesting indigenous plants and insects, including the carnivorous sundew plant and bog cotton. ⊗ *Peatland World, Lullymore • Map N5*

Rock of Dunamase

Left **Galway** Right **Lough Corrib**

Around Galway

COUNTY GALWAY HAS A PECULIAR MAJESTY *and an awesome sense of its closeness to nature, stalwartly facing the imposing Atlantic Ocean. Even the area around the county town, Galway City, squeezed onto a strip of land between the expanse of Lough Corrib and the immense waters of Galway Bay, possesses that same inspiring quality. As well as its own charms, with good restaurants and charming pubs, it is a good base from which to explore the area. South of the city is a gentler, greener countryside. While a good deal of the fascination of this southern edge of Galway lies simply in the tranquil landscape, for lovers of literature much of the interest is also in the connection with the romantic Irish poet WB Yeats (see p34). Although not originally from this region, Yeats returned often in his thoughts and in his work to the myths and grandeur of western Ireland, and spent many years living at his Thoor Ballylee near Gort, south of Galway City. Pleasant, gentle cruises on the lakes are another attraction.*

Kinvarra

🔟 Sights

1. Galway City
2. Lough Corrib
3. Kinvarra
4. Coole Park
5. Cong Abbey
6. Oughterard
7. Thoor Ballylee
8. Kilmacduagh
9. Spiddal
10. Athenry

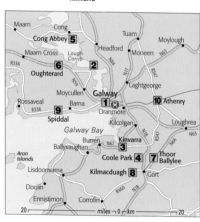

Galway City

Galway City

1 The pleasant, bustling regional capital started life as a fortress of the O'Connors of Connacht. Colonized in 1232 by Anglo-Normans, it became a prosperous seaport: some fine buildings survive, notably 16th-century Lynch's Castle (now a bank), and 14th-century St Nicholas's Church. A great atmosphere, with plenty of music and traditional shops. ⊗ *Map N2*

Lough Corrib

2 The vast expanse of Lough Corrib's cool waters, feeling more like part of the Atlantic Ocean than a lake, is Ireland's second largest, and a popular resort area for angling, boating and walking. ⊗ *Map N2*

Kinvarra

3 The little road around Galway Bay passes through a score of villages that are breathtaking in their prettiness and grandiose location. The most charming is Kinvarra, with its fishing harbour and pier cottages. It's the setting for a traditional music festival in May, and a fishing-boat gathering in August. ⊗ *Map N3*

Coole Park

4 The woods, lakes and paths of this national park and wildlife preserve, with its red deer and red squirrels, were once the grounds of a great Georgian mansion, home of Lady Augusta Gregory *(see p62)*. She hosted the most famous novelists and playwrights of her day and the Irish Revival began here. Names carved on the Autograph Tree include Shaw, Synge, Sean O'Casey and many more. The house itself fell into ruin and was dismantled. ⊗ *Gort • Map N3 • Open Apr–Sep: daily • Adm*

Cong Abbey

5 Poised on the narrow strip between Lough Corrib and Lough Mask, the attractive village of Cong lies just across the Galway border in County Mayo. Cong Abbey was an important Augustinian community founded by the King of Connacht in 1128 and became a leading spiritual centre. Closed down during the Reformation, it fell into ruin. What survives remains majestic; the cloisters have been partly reconstructed. ⊗ *Cong • Map M2*

Doorway, Cong Abbey

6 Oughterard

On the shores of Lough Corrib, this village has become a small resort area. Its chief prize, however, is Aughnanure Castle, beside the lake – a handsome remnant of a 16th-century tower-house of the O'Flaherties, the Connacht clan who terrified the ruling Anglo-Norman families of Galway. ◈ *Map N2 • Aughnanure Castle: Open May–mid-Jun & Oct: weekends; mid-Jun–Sep: daily • Adm*

7 Thoor Ballylee

Follow the sign "Yeats Tower" to reach the old tower-house in which WB Yeats and his wife Georgie spent much time during the 1920s. A sturdy little fortress, it was restored and converted by Yeats, and is described with touching detail in many of his poems. It is now lovingly preserved as a homage to Yeats. ◈ *Gort • Map N3 • Open Apr–Sep: 10am–6pm daily • Adm*

8 Kilmacduagh

An astonishing set of monastic ruins survives here. The original church established in AD 610 was enlarged over the centuries and replaced by a cathedral in the 14th century, though keeping many features of

Thoor Ballylee

the older buildings, including a 10th-century door. Around it are a number of other intriguing 13th- and 14th-century ecclesiastical buildings. There's also a Leaning Tower. ◈ *Gort • Map N3*

9 Spiddal

Officially Irish-speaking, and with a Gaelic summer school, Spiddal makes a pleasant stop on the Galway Bay coast road. Several craft workers have set up shop in the Spiddal Craft Village, where you can see pottery, weaving, knitting and other skilled work in progress, or buy the finished goods. ◈ *Map N2*

10 Athenry

The poignant folksong "The Fields of Athenry" (pronounced Athen-rye) gives little clue about this evocative reminder of the Anglo-Norman colonists. In 1211, Meiler de Bermingham made Athenry his seat, enclosed it with sturdy ramparts, built a little castle, and founded a Dominican Priory in 1241 where he and his descendants could be buried. Today, though damaged, much survives, together with a broken 15th-century cross erected in the central square. ◈ *Map N3*

To Be Carved

One of Yeats's poems is entitled *To Be Carved on a Stone at Thoor Ballylee*, and the words have indeed been carved at the house:
"I, the poet William Yeats
With old mill boards and sea-green slates
And smithy work from the Gorge forge
Restored this tower for my wife George;
And may these characteristics remain
When all is ruin once again".

Price Categories

For a three-course meal for one with half a bottle of wine (or equivalent meal), taxes and extra charges.	€ under €25
	€€ €25–€35
	€€€ €35–€55
	€€€€ €55–€70
	€€€€€ over €70

Above **Currarevagh House**

🔟 Places to Eat

1 Boluisce
This family-run restaurant has earned itself a high reputation for Connemara lamb, Irish beef, and delicious fish from the nearby Atlantic. ⊗ *Spiddal • Map N2 • 091 553286 • €€€*

2 Cre na Cille
Seafood, meat and game are the specialities of this excellent but unassuming family-run restaurant. It also has a large array of fine whiskeys. ⊗ *High St, Tuam • Map N2 • 093 28232 • €€€*

3 Paddy Burke's
The best time to visit this traditional pub is during Clarinbridge's September oyster festival. As well as shellfish from the famed local beds, it offers a choice of good meat and fish dishes. ⊗ *Clarinbridge • Map N2 • 091 796226 • Dis. access • €€€*

4 Currarevagh House
This restaurant is part of a country manor on the shores of Lough Corrib (famous for brown trout, which is on the menu in season). ⊗ *Oughterard • Map N2 • 091 552312 • €€€*

5 Nimmos
The Mediterranean cooking and live folk music on Wednesday and Saturday make this a popular place with locals. The walls are covered with *objets d'art* by the artist owner. ⊗ *Long Walk, Spanish Arch, Galway City • Map N2 • 091 561114 • €€€*

6 Cashel House
This country house and restaurant was once a gracious aristocratic home and has now earned itself international renown for both its food and atmosphere. ⊗ *Cashel • Map N2 • 095 31001 • €€€€*

7 O'Dowd's Seafood Bar and Restaurant
Beside Roundstone's pretty harbour, O'Dowd's serves steak and seafood dishes and does more for vegetarians than most Irish restaurants. ⊗ *Roundstone • Map N1 • 095 35809 • €€*

8 Aran Fisherman
This harbourside restaurant is certainly the best on the Aran Islands (where there is, admittedly, limited competition). Its seafood, caught the same day, must be the freshest in Ireland. ⊗ *Kilronan, Aran Islands • Map N1 • 099 61363 • €€€*

9 White Gables
In an informal whitewashed 19th-century inn, White Gables is best known for its lobster, but also serves other "surf and turf" dishes. ⊗ *Moycullen Village • Map N2 • 091 555744 • €€€*

10 McDonagh's Fish Restaurant
As you might expect, specializing mainly in seafood. Excellent seafood platter and friendly service. ⊗ *Kirwan's Lane, Galway City • Map N3 • 091 565001 • €€*

Note: *Unless otherwise stated, all restaurants accept credit cards and serve vegetarian meals*

Left **Clifden Bay** Right **Connemara National Park**

Connemara and Mayo

ONNEMARA – THE ROCKY MOUNTAINOUS COUNTRYSIDE *of western County Galway – is almost entirely uncultivated, a strange wilderness of water and stone, peat bog, headlands and barren hills. Along its shores, the Atlantic eats savagely into the land, making spectacular inlets and bays. Seemingly uninhabitable, in pre-famine days Connemara was crowded with poverty-stricken farmers, victims of the Protestant Ascendancy that had driven them from their farms across the Shannon. Thousands of rough dry-stone walls criss-cross the bare hills, enclosing their tiny abandoned fields. The famine wiped out most of Connemara's human life, and the memory of that disaster lingers sadly in the glorious landscape. The poignant scenery continues across Killary Fjord into County Mayo, where – as well as wide open spaces of bog, heath, mountain and lake – there are appealing small towns, a traditional way of life, and much to see.*

Detail, Westport House

Sights

1. Westport
2. Clifden
3. Kylemore Abbey
4. Connemara National Park and Twelve Bens Mountains
5. Sky Road
6. Roundstone
7. Leenane to Killary Harbour
8. Clare and Inishbofin Islands
9. Croagh Patrick
10. Céide Fields

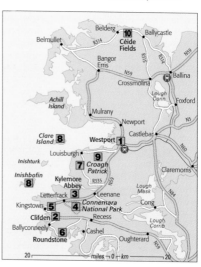

1 Westport

Busy, popular Westport is still small enough that countryside can be seen at the end of the main streets. Originally built in 1780 by the Earl of Altamont as an adjunct to his mansion Westport House, this is a good example of a planned town, with its dignified central Octagon and tree-lined Mall. It was all paid for by the slave-worked West Indian sugar plantations of the Earl's wife. Westport House remains imposing and grandly furnished, although touristy, with added attractions such as video games and an animal park. ◎ *Map M2* • *Westport House: Open Jun–Sep: daily (times vary); Adm*

2 Clifden

Regarded as the "capital" of Connemara, although hardly more than a village, this busy little resort lies among lovely green hills above Clifden Bay and at the foot of the Twelve Bens Mountains. A Georgian planned town built by John d'Arcy, it retains a certain character and style. At the end of summer, Clifden hosts the traditional Connemara Pony Show, which brings in hordes of horse-lovers. ◎ *Map M1*

3 Kylemore Abbey

The extraordinarily over-elaborate mock Gothic castle, built as a private house in 1868 for millionaire Mitchell Henry, has been a Benedictine convent since the 1920s. Although a religious community, it is also run as a commercial tourist attraction. The house and walled gardens are delightful, and the location magnificent, next to Kylemore Lough and with views towards the Twelve Bens. ◎ *Kylemore* • *Map M2* • *Open 9am–5:30pm daily* • *Adm*

4 Connemara National Park and Twelve Bens Mountains

Extending from Letterfrack village to the Twelve Bens, the park is a 5,000-acre conservation area of heath, bog and hills encompassing the grandest of Connemara's landscapes. The Twelve Bens, a dozen high peaks rising from the heart of the western mountains, dominate the Connemara skyline. A visitors' centre near the park entrance has a permanent exhibition on the flora, fauna, geology and history of the region. ◎ *Map M2* • *Visitors' Centre: Letterfrack; Open Mar–Oct: daily; Adm*

Kylemore Abbey

Grace O'Malley

Grace O'Malley (1530–1600) was the daughter of a Connacht chieftain. At 15, she married the O'Flaherty chief, whose men remained loyal to her after his death. With fortresses throughout Connacht, and based on Clare Island, in 1593 she visited Queen Elizabeth I, extracting a promise to be left in peace.

5 Sky Road

Named for its beautiful cliff-edge ocean views, the Sky Road is a 7-mile (11-km) loop that starts out from Clifden to skirt the narrow peninsula alongside Clifden Bay. Along the way it reaches empty beaches, wild hill scenery, and sights such as the ruins of Neo-Gothic Clifden Castle, the home of Clifden's founder John d'Arcy. ◈ *Map M1*

6 Roundstone

Cloch na Rón is the official name of this attractively laid out, Irish-speaking "planned village" built in the 1820s. In one way, it's an authentic, unpretentious lobster-fishing community, but it also has an arty side and many attractions for visitors, including a good beach, a range of eating places, galleries and traditional shops. ◈ *Map N2*

7 Leenane to Killary Harbour

The appealing village of Leenane lies beside the long, narrow inlet of Killary Fjord. From here, the dramatically beautiful road to the small oceanside resort of Louisburgh crosses the water between the peaks of Devil's Mother and Ben Gorm, and rises among lakes and streams along the narrow Delphi Valley, in places bursting with rhododendrons. One of the west's loveliest drives. ◈ *Map M2*

8 Clare and Inishbofin Islands

Dramatic Clare Island was the stronghold of Grace O'Malley, or Granuaile, whose little fortress still stands, as does the ruined abbey where she is buried. Inishbofin has a green, lonely beauty. Home of the O'Flaherty clan, and a hideaway of Grace O'Malley, it was taken by Cromwell. Both have small populations and prehistoric ruins. ◈ *Map M1*

9 Croagh Patrick

St Patrick supposedly climbed this black conical hill, one of Ireland's most sacred sites, dedicated to Lugh, God of Light. It is considered a pious act to make the steep climb on the rough, cutting stones to the summit (which gives phenomenal views). For the annual July pilgrimage, many ascend in bare feet. ◈ *Map M2*

10 Céide Fields

Preserved for thousands of years under a blanket of peat bog, the Céide site consists of walled fields cultivated in Stone Age times, together with stone ruins. All is explained by the excellent guided tours offered by the visitors' centre. ◈ *Map L2*

Croagh Patrick

Price Categories

For a three-course
meal for one with half
a bottle of wine (or
equivalent meal), taxes
and extra charges.

€ under €25
€€ €25–€35
€€€ €35–€55
€€€€ €55–€70
€€€€€ over €70

Above **Cashel House**

🔟 Places to Eat

1 O'Dowd's Seafood Bar and Restaurant

Beside Roundstone's pretty harbour, O'Dowds serves steak, chicken and seafood dishes and does more for vegetarians than most Irish restaurants. Bar snacks and daily specials as well as *à la carte* meals. ◈ *Roundstone • Map N1 • 095 35809 • Dis. access • €€*

2 Cashel House

This country house and restaurant has earned itself international renown for its food and atmosphere. Classic cooking and freshly caught local seafood. ◈ *Cashel • Map N2 • 095 31001 • €€€€*

3 Renvyle House

A gracious country house-style hotel on the shores of the Atlantic serving superb seafood, Connemara lamb, and a range of other classic Irish and European dishes. ◈ *Renvyle • Map M1 • 095 43511 • Dis. access • €€€€*

4 Asgard Tavern

An award-winning fisher-men's pub serves a good choice of seafood dishes. ◈ *The Quay, Westport • Map M2 • 098 25319 • Dis. access (bar only) • €€€*

5 Ardmore Country House and Restaurant

Using only local produce, this country house restaurant has earned itself renown for its wonderful steaks, lobster and oysters. ◈ *The Quay, Westport • Map M2 • 098 25994 • €€€*

6 Calveys Restaurant

By far the best place to eat on Achill Island, Calveys has an air of understated elegance and serves local fish and shellfish, free range poultry, organic vegetables and game. ◈ *Keel, Achill Island • Map M1 • 098 43158 • €€*

7 Quay Cottage

The best choice in town for vegetarian dishes, this harbour-side restaurant is also well known for its fresh fish, lobster, crab and steaks. ◈ *The Harbour, Westport • Map M2 • 098 26412 • Dis. access • €€€*

8 Newport House

This restaurant in a lovely Georgian mansion bases its menu on fresh produce from its own farm, gardens and fishery, and smokes its own salmon. Also has a superb wine cellar. ◈ *Newport • Map M2 • 098 41222 • Dis. access • €€€€*

9 Rosleague Manor

Connemara lamb and local seafood are specialities of the house, served with the best local ingredients. ◈ *Letterfrack • Map M2 • 095 41101 • €€*

10 Crockets on the Quay

Affordable, friendly and relaxed restaurant and bar on the quay, beside the River Moy. Choose from bar meals (great chowder) or a full menu featuring modern Irish cuisine. ◈ *Ballina • Map L2 • 096 75930 • Dis. access • €€€*

 Note: Unless otherwise stated, all restaurants accept credit cards and serve vegetarian meals

Left **Lough Swilly** Right **Hargadon's Pub, Sligo**

Yeats Country and the Northwest

THE NORTHWEST OF IRELAND IS AMONG THE LEAST EXPLORED *areas of the country, and yet it incorporates some of the finest and most dramatic scenery, with its beautiful, wide sandy beaches, towering mountains, woodland and forest parks. Driving is really the best way to tour this part of the country as public transport is all but non-existent, and it gives the visitor the freedom to explore at whim. The region's colloquial name is in honour of the two great Irish brothers, Jack B and WB Yeats, artist and poet respectively, who hailed from the ancient Celtic town of Sligo. This was also the legendary power base of the warrior Queen Maeve of Connaught and is packed with prehistoric sites. Donegal has played a more historic role throughout the centuries but was finally left isolated when it was excluded from the new Northern Ireland in 1921 (see p31). Its abandonment has left it with little in common with its fellow counties, historically or geographically.*

WB Yeats statue, Sligo

🔟 Sights

1. Inishowen Peninsula
2. Glenveagh National Park
3. Sligo
4. Horn Head
5. Lissadell & Drumcliffe
6. Loch Key & Boyle
7. Parkes Castle
8. Donegal
9. Killybegs
10. Letterkenny

Inishowen Peninsula
1 Undiscovered by so many, this glorious corner in the far northwest has possibly the finest scenery in Ireland, with the spectacular Slieve Snaght Mountain in the centre, Foyle and Swilly lakes to east and west, and the dune-fringed beaches facing the Atlantic. The peninsula also has its share of dramatic headlands and boasts Ireland's most northwesterly point at Malin Head. *Co Donegal • Map K4*

Glenveagh National Park
2 The extraordinary quartzite cone of Mount Errigal dominates the Derryveagh mountain range in this wild part of Donegal. It overlooks the Glenveagh National Park, which incorporates the beautiful Lough Veagh Valley, and Poisoned Glen. One theory behind the name is that British soldiers were fed Irish spurge, a poisonous plant indigenous to the area, to murder them. *Co Donegal • Map K4 • Open mid-Apr–Sep: 10:30am–6:30pm daily • Dis. access • Adm*

Sligo
3 This busy market town is home to the excellent Model Arts Centre, which incorporates the Niland Collection of Jack B Yeats's paintings, as well as quirky, arty shops, good bookshops and fine restaurants. To the east of town is the lovely Lough Gill, with a number of woodland walks. The brooding outline of Ben Bulben Mountain and the beaches of Strandhill and Rosses Point are only 10 minutes' drive away. *Co Sligo • Map L3*

Horn Head
4 This dramatic 180-m (600-ft) rockface is home to hundreds of seabirds, including guillemots, gulls and puffins, which swoop in and out of the crevices hewn into the rock. The headland is covered in purple heather and the views over the Atlantic are stupendous. *Co Donegal • Map K4*

Lissadell and Drumcliffe
5 Just north of Sligo is Drumcliffe church, where WB Yeats (*see p34*) is buried, and the visitors' centre focuses on items and books relating to the poet. The area was a great inspiration to Yeats and he was a frequent visitor at the rather forbidding Lissadell House a few miles to the west. Lissadell was home to the Gore-Booth family, who were active in the fight for Irish freedom. *Carney, Co Sligo • Map L3 • Lissadell House: Call for opening times 071 916 3150, Dis. access, Adm*

Lissadell House

Following pages: **Milk churns, rural Ireland**

6 Loch Key and Boyle
One of the best spots for viewing this magnificent lake is from the main Sligo-to-Boyle road. The Loch Key Forest Park has numerous walks along the lakeside and through the woods. Boyle is an appealing nearby town with a ruined abbey, interesting museum and some fine Georgian architecture. ◈ *Co Roscommon • Map M3*

7 Parke's Castle
Built by a Captain Robert Parke in 1609, and overlooking Lough Gill, this fortified manor house was erected on the site of an earlier tower house. The foundations and moat of this earlier structure are incorporated into the castle but otherwise it is a fine example of a plantation house. You can visit the castle by road or by boat on the Lough Gill cruise. ◈ *Nr Dromahair, Co Leitrim • Map L3 • Open mid-Mar–Oct: 10am–6pm daily; last adm 5:15pm • Adm*

Parke's Castle

St Eunan's Cathedral, Letterkenny

8 Donegal
Donegal is most famous for its tweed production *(see p125)* with Magee's the biggest manufacturer based here. The Diamond, a triangular central market, is at the heart of the town and an obelisk in the centre commemorates four Franciscans who wrote *Annals of the Four Masters* in the 1630s. This extraordinary opus follows the history of the Gaelic people from the Great Flood up to the 17th century. ◈ *Co Donegal • Map L4*

9 Killybegs
An exciting place to be when the boats come in, Killybegs is one of the busiest fishing ports in the country. As the trawlers unload their catches gulls squawk over the water in an attempt to claim a discarded morsel. ◈ *Co Donegal • Map L3*

10 Letterkenny
Donegal's largest town is flanked by the Derryveagh Mountains to the west and the Sperrin Mountains to the east. Its main street, said to be the longest in Ireland, is overlooked by the Neo-Gothic St Eunan's Cathedral. The County Museum has a good display on local history. ◈ *Co Donegal • Map K4*

Above **Hargadon's**

Price Categories

For a three-course meal for one with half a bottle of wine (or equivalent meal), taxes and extra charges.

Places to Eat and Drink

1 Cromleach Lodge
Signposted from the N4 at Castlebaldwin, this restaurant and country house has beautiful views of Lough Arrow mountains. Eating here is a gourmet experience with simple dishes expertly prepared. ◎ *Ballindoon, Boyle, Co Sligo • Map M3 • 071 916 5155 • Closed L • Dis. access • €€€€*

2 Rathmullan House
A grand country house hotel, this could be described as an institution in Donegal. Gourmet dinners are served in the Pavilion, a conservatory-type room maximizing natural light. ◎ *Rathmullan, Co Donegal • Map L3 • 074 915 8117 • Dis. access • €€€€*

3 The Fleet Inn
The restaurant above this busy pub, right in the centre of Killybegs, makes the very best use of the freshest fish. ◎ *Killybegs, Co Donegal • Map L3 • 074 973 1518 • €€€*

4 McGroarty's
This popular pub offers excellent and imaginative dishes, highly praised by locals and visitors alike. ◎ *The Diamond, Donegal • Map L4 • 074 972 1049 • Closed D • Dis. access • €*

5 Yeats's Tavern
This large, bustling tavern is a popular stopping place on the way to Donegal. Generous helpings and a huge choice. ◎ *Drumcliffe, Co Sligo • Map L3 • 071 916 3117 • €–€€*

6 Gavarogue
Sophisticated and understated bar-restaurant beside the river. The excellent cooking is modern Irish. ◎ *15–16 St Stephen St, Sligo, Co Sligo • Map L3 • 071 914 0100 • Dis. access • €€€*

7 Kealey's Seafood Bar
Beside the pier, this atmospheric restaurant-bar serves first-class seafood and a range of meat and vegetarian dishes. Traditional music most Sundays. ◎ *Greencastle, Co Donegal • Map K5 • 074 938 1010 • €€€*

8 Hargadon's Pub
An institution in Sligo, this is a real old-fashioned, dark-beamed pub. There's a warren of rooms with benched snugs giving privacy and atmosphere. Good, hearty pub food. ◎ *Sligo, Co Sligo • Map L3 • 071 917 0933 • €€*

9 Golf Club
The position of this clubhouse is worth a visit just for the view, but the food is excellent too. Fill up on delicious fresh seafood, then walk it off along the sandy beach. ◎ *Strandhill, Co Sligo • Map L3 • 071 916 8188 • €€*

10 Smuggler's Creek
Take a table with a view in this family-run restaurant overlooking the sweep of Donegal Bay. The speciality is seafood but they also provide a good range of other dishes. ◎ *Rossnowlagh, Co Donegal • Map L3 • 071 985 2366 • €€€*

 Note: *Unless otherwise stated, all restaurants accept credit cards and serve vegetarian meals*

Left **Mount Stewart** Right **Derry**

Northern Ireland

THE BRITISH ENCLAVE WHICH REMAINED IN IRELAND, *after the rest of the country became independent in 1921, blends the two nations of which it is a part. A distinctive society has developed here, especially the historic cultural divide between Nationalists (Catholics of Irish descent) and Loyalists (Protestants of English and Scottish descent) – each group has its own traditions. Yet between Northern Ireland and the Republic there are more similarities than differences, from music, to food and drink, to the landscape – indeed, some of the north's scenery is among the best in the country.*

Ulster-American Folk Park

🔟 Sights

1. Castle Coole
2. Giant's Causeway
3. Mount Stewart
4. Glens of Antrim
5. Lower Loch Erne
6. Armagh
7. Belfast
8. Ulster-American Folk Park & Ulster History Park
9. Florence Court
10. Derry

Castle Coole

1 The mansion built in the 1790s for the Earl of Belmore by James Wyatt stands grandly at the end of a long driveway and is set in impressive grounds. The house has been almost completely rebuilt in its original Neo-Classical style as commissioned by the first earl, while the sumptuous interior is richly decorated with elaborate plasterwork. The lavish 18th- and 19th-century Regency furnishings are those favoured by the second earl during the 1820s. *Nr Enniskillen • Map L4 • 028 6632 2690 • Open Easter–May & Sep: 1–6pm Sat–Sun; May–Aug: 1–6pm Fri–Wed • Adm*

Giant's Causeway

2 The Causeway, a designated a World Heritage Site since 1986, is a truly remarkable natural spectacle, its thousands of extraordinary hexagonal pillars of basalt rock clustered like a gigantic piece of honeycomb. The rocks descend from seafront cliffs into the water and disappear from view. Supposedly created by legendary warrior Finn MacCoul as his stepping stones to Scotland *(see p38)*, the Causeway was really created by a volcanic eruption 60 million years ago. There's a useful visitors' centre nearby. *Map K5*

Giant's Causeway

Mount Stewart

3 The grandly aristocratic 18th-century home of the Marquises of Londonderry displays a superb art collection, and stands in wonderful landscaped gardens with remarkable plant collections. There is some extraordinary topiary, exquisite planned views and numerous odd stonecarvings representing creatures such as dodos and dinosaurs. Also in the grounds is the elegant octagonal Temple of the Winds, a copy of a Classical relic near Athens. *Strangford Lough, near Newtownards • Map L6 • 028 4278 8387 • House: Open Apr–Sep: noon–6pm daily (closed Tue, May & Sep); Gardens: May–Sep: 10am–8pm daily; Oct–Apr: 10am–4pm daily • Adm*

Glens of Antrim

4 Among the finest scenery in Ireland is the coast of County Antrim, where nine beautiful valleys (glens) cut deeply through high rolling hills to descend grandly into the sea. The effect, seen from the shore road, is spectacular. Follow the A2 through Carnlough, with its tiny harbour, through Waterfoot, with waterfalls and a Forest Park, all the way up to the Giant's Causeway. *Map K5*

Lower Loch Erne

5 The serene waters and small islands extending north from Enniskillen can be explored by boat, or encircled by road. Devenish Island, reached from the east bank, is the remarkable site of 6th-century monastic ruins, a Celtic High Cross, and an 80-ft (25-m) Round Tower. Boa Island, reached by a causeway, is noted for a strange double-faced Celtic stone carving. Another group of curious stone figures stands on White Island. *Map L4*

Armagh

Around Ireland – Northern Ireland

Armagh

Armagh

Armagh

Armagh
6 The city where Queen Macha built her fortress some 3,000 years ago, Armagh has a curious role in Ulster's religious divide. St Patrick based himself here, and the city is considered the ecclesiastical capital of both communities, with a Catholic and a Protestant cathedral, each dedicated to Patrick. The town also has a good museum and astronomy centre. ◈ *Map L5*

Belfast
7 Northern Ireland's capital is a vibrant Victorian city with good shops, pubs, museums and galleries. Call at the Belfast Welcome Centre for details of the attractions in and around the city. ◈ *Map L6 • Belfast Welcome Centre: Royal Ave; Open daily.*

Ulster-American Folk Park and Ulster History Park
8 Many Americans can trace their roots back to 19th-century rural Ulster, and many, like local-born millionaire Thomas Mellon, did very well in their new home. The Folk Park, built around Mellon's birthplace, reconstructs their lives on both sides of the Atlantic. The nearby History Park tells the region's rich story from the Stone Age up to the Protestant Plantation. ◈ *Near Omagh • Map L4 • Open Apr–Sep: daily; Oct–Mar: Mon–Fri • Adm*

The Six Counties
The nine counties of the Kingdom of Ulster were the last part of Ireland to be subdued by the English. Its conquest in 1607 led to an exodus of Irish nobility, whose lands were "planted" with British Protestants. When the War of Independence created the Irish Republic, six of the Ulster counties remained British under the name Northern Ireland.

Florence Court
9 The gardens and grandiose 18th-century Palladian mansion originally belonged to Lord Mountflorence. Among the original features are an icehouse and a water-driven sawmill, while the interior is decorated with ornamental plasterwork and period furnishings. ◈ *A32, near Enniskillen • Map L4 • Open Apr & Sep: 1–6pm Sat-Sun; May–Aug: 1–6pm Wed–Mon • Adm*

Derry
10 At the heart of Derry (Londonderry) is a fascinating walled Plantation town, its 350-year-old fortifications almost intact. Free Derry Corner, where a wall is painted with the words "You Are Now Entering Free Derry", is the most famous of the town's many political murals. ◈ *Map K4*

City Hall, Belfast

Price Categories

For a three-course meal for one with half a bottle of wine (or equivalent meal), taxes and extra charges.

£	under £25
££	£25–£35
£££	£35–£55
££££	£55–£70
£££££	over £70

Above **Crown Liquor Saloon**

🔟 Places to Eat

1 Shanks Restaurant
Holder of a Michelin star, Shanks Rrestaurant is designed by Sir Terence Conran and is decorated with paintings by David Hockney. Menus change monthly. *Blackwood Golf Centre, 150 Crawfordsburn Rd, Bangor • Map K6 • 02891 853313 • Dis. access • £££*

2 Cayenne
Lively and different, Cayenne's menu comes from all over the world and the atmosphere attracts a fashionable clientele. *7 Lesley House, Shaftesbury Sq, Belfast • Map L6 • 028 9033 1532 • Dis. access • £££*

3 The Morning Star
This historic 19th-century pub-restaurant hosts gourmet nights every month and always features fine local seafood, meat and poultry. *17–19 Pottinger's Entry, Belfast • Map L6 • 028 9023 5986 • £*

4 Crown Liquor Saloon
Local favourites are served at this lovely old pub, such as Irish stew with champ – buttery mashed potatoes and spring onions. *46 Great Victoria St, Belfast • Map K6 • 028 9027 9901 • £*

5 Pier 36
This award-winning pub serves great seafood and local game, and bakes its own bread on a range right in the middle of the dining area. *The Parade, Donaghadee • Map K6 • 028 9188 4466 • Dis. access • £*

6 Nick's Warehouse
Nick and Cathy Price's beautifully converted warehouse restaurant can be found on Belfast's cobbled streets and has a great atmosphere. *35–9 Hill Street, Belfast • Map L6 • 028 9043 9690 • Dis. access • ££*

7 The Portaferry Hotel
This restaurant on the shores of Strangford Lough has a high reputation for top-quality shellfish and other seafood, most of it from the waters of the lake. *The Strand, Portaferry • Map L6 • 028 4272 8231 • Dis. access • ££*

8 Bushmills Inn
In the village that produces Ulster's finest whiskey is an atmospheric re-creation of an old coaching inn, with open fires and gas lighting. The menu ranges from local beef to fresh salmon. *25 Main St, Bushmills • Map K6 • 028 2073 2339 • Dis. access • ££*

9 The Quays Bar and Restaurant
Fresh seafood is the main attraction at this affordable and friendly eating spot. *New Harbour Rd, Portavogie • Map K6 • 028 4277 2225 • Dis. access • £*

10 The Lobster Pot
Unsurprisingly best known for its lobster and other seafood, but also has a wide menu of European and Irish treats. *The Square, Strangford • Map K6 • 028 4488 1288 • £££*

 Note that, unlike the rest of Ireland, the currency in Northern Ireland has not changed to the euro but remains pounds sterling.

STREETSMART

DUBLIN'S TOP 10

Left **Dublin Airport** Right **Ferry, Dun Laoghaire**

🔟 Getting to Dublin

1 By Air from the UK

British Airways, Aer Lingus and low-cost airlines such as Ryanair run regular flights to Dublin and all major Irish cities. They depart from London's five airports (Heathrow, City, Gatwick, Luton and Stansted) and from 15 other UK cities including Birmingham, Leeds and Glasgow, as well as the Isle of Man and the Channel Islands. 🚫 *Aer Lingus: 01-886 8888, www.aerlingus.com • British Airways: 1-800 626747, www.britishair ways.com • Ryanair: 01-609 7800, www.ryanair.com*

2 By Air from Europe

Flights from most major cities in Europe go direct to Dublin, although some connections are seasonal. Out of season flights are via London, Amsterdam or Paris. All travellers from Australasia have to fly to Dublin via Europe.

3 By Air from North America

Aer Lingus and Delta Air Lines fly direct from various locations in the USA to Dublin, and to Shannon in the southwest. 🚫 *Delta Air Lines: 1-800 768080, www.delta.com*

4 Internet Bargains

Most airlines now have their own websites for booking flights and will have details of last-minute bargains and general availability. Ryanair has some very cheap deals, with flights from some UK and European cities for as little as €12.

5 Dublin Airport

Dublin Airport is 12 km (7 miles) from the city centre and has recently been enlarged and upgraded, easing overcrowding. 🚫 *Dublin Airport: 01-814 1111, www.dublinairport.com*

6 Airport–City Connections

Journey time varies, depending on traffic – morning and evening rush hours are best avoided. Airlink is an express bus service between the airport and the city's main bus and rail stations. Buses run every 10 minutes from early morning to midnight; journey time is 40 minutes. Aircoach (5:30am–10:30pm) picks up at various points in the city, costing €6. Tickets for both can be bought on board. Taxis cost around €18–20. 🚫 *Airlink: 01-873 4222, www.dublinbus.ie • Aircoach: 01-844 7118, www.aircoach.ie*

7 By Ferry from the UK

Irish Ferries operate a cruise and fast ferry service from Holyhead in Wales to Dublin Port; Stena Line operates its High Speed Superferry from Holyhead to Dun Laoghaire and a cruise ferry to Dublin Port. Crossing time is between 90 minutes and 3.5 hours. Norse Merchant Ferries runs a service from Liverpool to Dublin Port. There are good transport links to the centre from both ports. 🚫 *Irish Ferries: 01-661 0715, www. irishferries.com • Stena Line: 01-204 7777, www. stenaline.co.uk • Norse Merchant Ferries: 01-819 2999, www.norse merchantferries.com*

8 By Ferry from Europe

Brittany Ferries runs a cruise service from Roscoff (22 hours) in France to Cork *(see p90)*. 🚫 *Brittany Ferries: 021-427 7801, 08705-360360 (UK) www.brittanyferries.com*

9 By Bus and Coach

Various companies run services to Dublin and other Irish cities. Bus Eireann and Eurolines offer a day and night service from London via Holyhead. Journey time is 11–13 hours. 🚫 *Bus Eireann: 01-836 6111, www. buseireann.ie • Eurolines: www.eurolines.com*

10 By Train

Train-and-ferry journey time is much quicker than by coach but, with bargain airfares available, neither may be an economical alternative. 🚫 *National Rail Enquiry Service: www.rail.co.uk; www.irishrail.ie*

Left **Dublin Bus** Centre **Parking sign** Right **DART electric train**

Getting Around Dublin

1 City Buses
Dublin Bus runs a comprehensive network around the city, every 10–20 minutes from 6am to 11:30pm. All buses operate an autofare system so make sure you have change or a travel pass. One-day, three-day, five-day, weekly or monthly travel passes are available from tourist centres and some newsagents. Nitelink Buses operate every 20 minutes from 12:30am to 2am Monday to Wednesday, and from 12:30am to 4:30am Thursday to Saturday from Westmoreland Street, D'Olier Street, College Green, St Stephen's Green and O'Connell Street. Travel passes are not valid on these buses, which have a flat charge of €4–6. Green and cream bus stops are for the Hop-On-Hop-Off tourist buses and are situated at 16 major tourist points around the city. ✆ *Dublin Bus: 01-873 4222, www.dublinbus.ie*

2 DART
DART (Dublin Area Rapid Transport) is an electric train service covering 28 stations from picturesque Malahide and Howth to the north of the city to Greystones in County Wicklow, with a few city centre stops. The last train leaves the town centre at 11:30pm. ✆ *DART: 01-836 6222, www.irishrail.ie*

3 Luas
A new light railway system is currently under construction in Dublin. The first three lines (A: Tallaght to Abbey Street; B: Sandyford to St Stephen's Green; and C: Abbey Street to Connolly Station) are due to open in 2004. A fourth line, B1, from Sandyford to Cherrywood, and a fifth, from Connolly Station to Docklands, are in the pipeline. ✆ *Luas: www.luas.ie*

4 Walking
The centre of Dublin is compact and easy to walk around, and increasing numbers of streets are being pedestrianized.

5 Taxis
Taxi ranks can be found at the airport, main stations, large hotels and a few designated areas around the city. Fares are metered, with the base rate around €3. Taxis can be hailed in the street. ✆ *Access/Metro cabs: 01-668 3333 • National Radio Cabs: 01-677 2222*

6 Rental Cars
All the main car rental companies have desks at the airport and in the city. A full driving licence is required and age restriction is generally between 23 and 70 years. Rental usually includes unlimited mileage and third party fire and theft insurance. ✆ *Murrays/Europcar: 01-614 2800, www.europcar.ie*

7 Road Rules
City and town speed limits are 50 kmph, outskirts are 80 kmph, with 100 kmph on open roads and 120 kmph on motorways. Speed cameras are in frequent use and on-the-spot fines can be issued by the police. Road signs come in both English and Irish and kilometres and miles.

8 Petrol Stations
Most rental cars now take unleaded fuel, but leaded and diesel are also available. The nearest petrol stations to the centre are at Ballsbridge, Donnybrook and Usher's Quay.

9 Parking
There is plenty of parking available in the centre, with electronic signs at various strategic points giving up-to-the-minute availability of spaces. Clamping is in operation throughout Dublin for illegal parking.

10 Trains
Ireland's train service is operated by Irish Rail (Iarnrod Eireann), with trains to most cities and main towns. Direct services are efficient but some areas such as Donegal *(see p112)* are not served by the railway and there are no coastal routes in the south, east or north, so these areas must be explored by car or bus. ✆ *Irish Rail: www.irishrail.ie*

Streetsmart

Left **Irish Tourist Board logo** Centre **Irish-English sign** Right **Driving in Dublin**

Sources of Information

1 Irish Tourist Board
The main tourist office in Dublin is very helpful with information on tourist sights, hotel accommodation and any other visitors' needs.
Irish Tourist Board: Baggot St Bridge • 1850 230330 • www.ireland-travel.ie

2 Discounts and Concessions
There are reductions on entrance tickets to many historic sites and attractions, on some transport, and even on some accommodation and travel packages within Ireland, for students, children, the unemployed, senior citizens and families. Carry appropriate photo ID. To visit several sights at a discount, buy a Heritage Card (see p124).

3 Business Hours
Most shops and businesses are open 9am to 5pm, Monday to Friday. Banks open Monday to Friday 10am to 4pm (sometimes until 5pm on Thursday); post offices Monday to Friday 9am to 5:30pm, Saturday 9am to 12:30pm. Pubs open Monday to Thursday 10:30am to 11:30pm, Friday to Saturday 10:30am to 12:30am, Sunday 12:30pm to 11pm.

4 Internet
Ireland is fully online, with cyber cafés in most towns, and several in Dublin. Charges are generally around €2 for 15 minutes. Public libraries also offer Internet access. Most major attractions have their own websites.

5 Driving
Ireland has one of the highest percentages of driving fatalities in Europe. Drink-driving is a problem and speed limits are often ignored, though a new "penalty points" system is improving the situation. Congestion in towns is high, but rural roads are relatively traffic-free. Even main roads may have only two lanes – pull onto the hard-shoulder to let others overtake. Speed limits are 120 kmph (74mph) on motorways, 100 kmph (62 mph) on main roads, 50 kmph (31 mph) in towns. Drive on the left. Yellow lines indicate parking restrictions. All types of fuel are available.

6 Road Signs
Ireland uses Europe's international pictorial system of road signs. Confusing signs that give two alternative routes to the same place without stating the distances are commonplace in rural Ireland. When given, distances may be approximate. Officially, the Republic uses kilometres (green signs), but many roadsigns are in miles (white signs). Often, place names are given in Irish and English.

7 Climate
The weather in Ireland is wet and mild all year round, but generally without extremes. It rarely freezes except on uplands, while summer can see some hot spells.

8 Embassies and Consulates
Britain and the US both have embassies in Dublin (see box). Most other countries have an embassy or consulate in the city – consult the Yellow Pages.

9 Tipping
Service charges of 10–15 per cent are added to bills in hotels and restaurants. Tip taxi drivers around 10 per cent, porters 50 cents or €1. Bar staff need not be tipped.

10 Northern Ireland
The border crossing between the Republic and Northern Ireland is normally simple, with few formalities. However, check with car rental companies that you may take the vehicle across the border, which is still a national frontier.

Embassies
British Embassy
29 Merrion Rd • Map G5 • 01 205 3700

US Embassy
42 Elgin Rd, Ballsbridge • Bus Nos. 7, 8 • 01 668 8777

Opening times of museums and other sights vary and are given next to their appropriate entries in this guide.

Left **Rush-hour traffic** Right **Boarding an Irish bus**

10 Things to Avoid

1 Drink-driving
There are very strict drink-driving laws in Ireland and you can be stopped and breathalysed at any time. Within the city, most places can be reached on foot, and restaurants are very happy to call cabs.

2 Unsafe Areas
It is unwise to wander around any badly lit areas of any city at night, and Dublin is no exception. It is also advisable not to walk around on your own late at night. There are areas of the city that have a reputation for being more dangerous than others – the northside is a bit rough after dark, so stick to the main thoroughfares such as O'Connell Street *(see p61)* and the quays. On the southside, around Dolphin's Barn, beyond Portobello, is a notorious area for drug-related crime, so avoid that both day and night, and similarly Summerhill off Gardiner Street on the northside. However neither of these areas has anything to draw the tourist so you are unlikely to find yourself there unless lost.

3 Carrying Valuables
It is always a mistake to carry valuables around with you when you're sightseeing, so leave them in the hotel safe. If you're driving, never leave anything visible in the car to tempt a break-in. Like any capital city, beware of pickpockets. Don't put temptation in their way by leaving bags open and valuables visible.

4 Rush Hour Traffic
The traffic has got much worse in Dublin over the last few years and the rush hour lasts from about 8–9:30am and 5–7pm so allow extra time if you need to travel between these times. This is particularly important on the route to the airport, on which traffic problems are currently exacerbated by the building of the Port Tunnel.

5 Theft
Dublin's pub culture is a major part of its charm and character, but when pubs become crowded they are a haven for petty thieves. Keep your money in your bag and your bag on your lap or where you can see it at all times. Even better, wear a money belt.

6 Drinking in Hotels
It is best to avoid drinking in hotel bars unless money is no object. Prices are always higher than in local bars and pubs, and a gratuity may be added.

7 Taxis
There has been a problem with a lack of taxis around the city for late-night revellers. If you are at a restaurant or club ask the waiter to call for one rather than trying your luck on the street. Recent deregulation may improve the situation and hopefully bring more cabs onto the street.

8 Parking Fines
Dublin's traffic wardens are very sharp and quite thick on the ground, so make sure you don't overrun your time as you'll be fined immediately. Clampers are also about all over the city, and it is time-consuming and expensive to get released.

9 International Rugby Weekends
From January to May the Six Nations Cup is played out between Italy, Wales, Scotland, Ireland, France and England with matches in the various countries. These weekends are best avoided, unless you're a rugby fan – hotel prices increase and the city is overcrowded.

10 Countrywide Public Transport
The public transport system around Ireland is generally poor *(see p121)*. There is a rail service to the main cities from Dublin but it is difficult to tour from one place to another as rail and bus links are limited. If you need to use public transport make sure you have researched your route beforehand.

Left **Heritage Card** Right **Dublin bicycles**

Dublin on a Budget

1 Sightseeing for Free

Most of the properties owned and run by Duchas, the State Heritage Service, are reasonably priced, while all national museums, galleries and libraries are free. There is a minimal charge for entry to some city churches but around the country they are generally free.

2 Sightseeing at a Discount

Sights and museums are either privately or state-run so discounts vary from site to site. On average, the concessions given for children, over 60s and students work out at about one third of the price of the full adult ticket. If you are planning to visit a number of historic sights, it is worth investing in a Heritage Card costing around €20 for adults and €7.50 for children and students. It is valid for one year from the date of purchase. You can buy the card at the first Duchas site you visit or send for one from their website. The National Trust offers a similar deal for properties in Northern Ireland. Duchas: www.heritageireland.ie • National Trust: www.national trust.org.uk

3 Discount Travel Cards

Youth and student discounts are available on presentation of an International Student ID Card (ISIC) for some museums, and rail and bus travel. Train discount cards include Irish Rail's Irish Rover card, but you need to be covering quite a distance to make it worthwhile. The most useful in Ireland is the combined bus and rail pass, the Irish Explorer Ticket. It covers all Intercity train and bus lines and the DART in Dublin (see p121).

4 Cheap Eateries

There is no shortage of these in the city, including McDonald's and Burger King, Beshoffs for fish and chips and a limitless supply of cafés and juice bars. Most small towns have a take-away of some description and garages and Spar shops throughout the country usually have a hot food counter. You can also get take-aways from some supermarkets.

5 Bicycle Hire

This is a cheap and fast way of getting about and Dublin is small enough for this to be a sensible option. However, few companies now rent bikes, due to insurance costs. Irish Cycling Safaris is based in Belfield university campus. Charges range from about €18 per day to €80 per week. Bikes are easy to steal so make sure you have a good padlock and chain. Irish Cycling Safaris: 260 0749

6 Cross-Country Buses

Ireland's public transport network is not brilliant (see p121). Trains link the main towns and cities but getting from one regional town to another is not easy. On intercity routes it is much cheaper to go by bus.

7 Hostel Accommodation

There are numerous hostels around the country. Many of the Dublin ones are of a good quality and you can get single and even double rooms at very low prices.

8 Big Breakfasts

The full Irish breakfast in hotels is a huge affair and will set you up for the day.

9 Off-season Travel

Travelling out of season and avoiding special weekends will save you money. Prices are hiked up during Rugby International weekends (see p123), St Patrick's weekend (see p41) and other bank holidays. In winter there are excellent hotel deals.

10 Shopping Carefully

Many items are no cheaper in Ireland than elsewhere, including tweeds. Seek out markets and craft shops where you could pick up original items for much less than in stores.

 Another option for cheap accommodation in Ireland are the universities during student holiday times.

Left **Celtic Claddagh ring** Centre **Aran jersey** Right **Enamel brooch**

Things to Buy

1 Linen
Ireland is world famous for its linen and there are some beautiful, original designs to be found. There is usually a selection on offer in most tourist shops. The choice includes embroidered bedcovers and table-cloths, linen pillowcases and duvet covers. At the less grand end of the scale, small embroidered handkerchiefs make good gifts and tea towels can be found everywhere.

2 Woollen Jerseys
Ireland is justly renowned for its terrific jerseys, and the Aran is the most famous. It can be fun to buy them in the west of Ireland if you're travelling around, although the range is probably better in Dublin. The larger department stores, specialist jersey outlets and tourist shops are the best places to try.

3 Ceramics
There are a number of excellent contemporary pottery companies available in most of the larger department stores such as Brown Thomas or Avoca Handweavers *(see p75)*. But search out craft shops for original pieces by individuals.

4 Tweed
One of the most famous tweed-producing areas is Donegal *(see p112)* where tweed can be bought either ready-made as clothing or off the bale as lengths of cloth. Hats and waist-coats are popular and come in a variety of tweeds. Most smaller items are widely available in tourist shops, but for the full tweed suit you'd be better off with the specialist. Try Kevin and Howlin *(see p57)*.

5 Jewellery
You can find Celtic jewellery in some form or another all over the city, but be careful of the quality. For the best in traditional and contemporary jewellery go to Whichcraft in Temple Bar *(see p19)*. This will give you an idea of top quality and prices. If you're feeling adventurous you can commission a piece. There is a huge variety on offer all over the country, from ancient Celtic to modern designs.

6 Musical Instruments
The penny whistle is one of the most commonly found traditional Irish musical instruments and cheap replicas can be found all over the city. Enquire in a proper music shop if you are looking for a decent one. The *bodhrán* is a goatskin handheld drum; this too is widely reproduced but the good ones need to be specially sought out. Handmade harps are a particular speciality in Dublin and Mayo.

7 Smoked Salmon
Irish smoked salmon is world famous and is widely exported. Much of it is farmed these days so seek out wild salmon; the taste is far superior. Wrights of Howth *(see p75)* has outlets at the airport and at Howth, but most fishmongers stock wild salmon.

8 Whiskey
Jamesons *(see p63)* is probably the best known Irish brand and is a fine smooth blend; Bushmills is also a popular whiskey produced in the north. For everyday whiskey drinking the average Irish person would probably settle for Powers – an altogether rougher experience.

9 Crystal and Glassware
Waterford Crystal is the best known producer of glassware in Ireland *(see p83)* but other quality producers exist. Galway Irish Crystal and Tipperary Crystal are two contenders, with Jerpoint Glass tending towards contemporary design.

10 Chocolates and Cheese
The Irish are very good at producing chocolates and the leading brand names are Bewley's and Lir. Ireland is also famous for its cheeses. Cashel Blue, Doolin and Durrus are only a few of a large number worth sampling.

POST TELECOM EIREANN

Left **Irish post sign** Right **Irish Telecom sign**

Banking and Communications

1 Banks

Allied Irish Bank (AIB), the Bank of Ireland, the Ulster Bank, the National Irish Bank, and the TSB are the five retail banks in the Republic. They are open Monday to Friday, 10am to 4pm. ATMs (cashpoints) are located outside most banks in the city, and are the fastest and cheapest way to get local currency, drawing money directly from your account, if you belong to a co-operating bank. All UK cashcards can be used at these machines.

2 Currency

Ireland joined the European Monetary Union in 1999, with 11 other EU countries, and the euro has been the sole legal tender since early 2002. Coin denominations are 1, 2, 5, 10, 20 and 50 cents, while notes come in denominations of 5, 10, 20, 50, 100, 200 and 500 euros. There are 100 cents to 1 euro.

3 Credit Cards and Travellers' Cheques

Visa and MasterCard are the most widely accepted cards; American Express and Diners Club less so. You can withdraw cash from ATMs using credit cards. Travellers' cheques are still the safest way to carry money but the rise of ATMs is fast supplanting the need for them.

4 Exchanging Money

For all foreign currencies outside of the EMU, the banks offer the best rates of exchange. Bureaux de change rates vary but they are likely to be better than hotel rates if the banks are closed. Some department stores offer exchange facilities.

5 Post

Most post offices open from 9am to 5:30pm Monday to Friday and 9am to 1pm, 2:15pm to 5pm on Saturdays. The General Post Office in O'Connell Street *(see p62)* is open all day, seven days a week, but stamps can also be purchased from some newsagents and shops. Post boxes in Ireland are green. The easiest way to receive mail in Dublin is to have it sent to your hotel but a *poste restante* service is also available from major post offices.

6 Telephones

The majority of phone booths are controlled by Telecom Eireann (Eircom). Public payphones are easy to find and the wording around the top of each booth indicates whether it takes coins, phonecards or credit cards – most in Dublin are now card-operated. The cheapest time to make calls is after 6pm and at weekends. Calls made from hotels can be expensive.

7 Phonecards

Pre-paid phonecards, available in several denominations, are useful for long distance calls. These, as well as card-credits for mobile phones, can be bought at newsagents, post offices, supermarkets and other retail outlets.

8 Internet

You can find an Internet café in most areas of Dublin and some hotels also offer Internet facilities. Failing that, try the nearest public library or post office.

9 Newspapers

The Republic of Ireland has six national daily papers and five Sunday papers. Quality dailies include the *Irish Times*, the *Irish Independent* and the *Examiner*. Ireland's daily tabloid is the *Star* and the evening paper is the *Evening Herald*. All British papers are on sale throughout Dublin and larger newsagents stock international newspapers.

10 Radio and Television

Ireland has four television channels: RTE 1, Network 2, TV3 and TG4. There are six national radio stations including an Irish language service, and many local ones. The five British channels can be picked up through cable and satellite connections.

Left **Pharmacy sign** Centre **Police station sign** Right **Police car**

Security and Health

1 Emergency numbers

Dial 999 or 112 in an emergency and you will be connected to the service you require – police, fire, ambulance or coastguard.

2 Police

The police force in the Irish Republic is called the *Garda Siochana*. An individual male police officer is called a *garda* and a female police officer is called a *bean garda*.

3 Hospitals

Beaumont, St James's and St Vincent's hospitals all have a 24-hour accident and emergency department. Dublin Dental Hospital serves emergency dental needs and the Eye and Ear Royal Victoria Hospital has an out-patient surgery every day. ✆ *Beaumont Hospital: Beaumont Rd, Dublin 9, 01-809 2714 • St James's Hospital: St James's St, Dublin 8, 01-416 2775 • St Vincent's University Hospital: Elm Park, Dublin 4, 01-209 4504/4387 • Dublin Dental Hospital: Lincoln Place, Dublin 2, 01-612 7200 • Eye & Ear Hospital: Adelaide Rd, Dublin 2, 01-664 4600*

4 Medical Charges

EU visitors can claim free medical treatment in the Republic of Ireland if they have a form E111 from their own country, available at post offices. To avoid paying for any treatments or prescribed medicines in the event of serious illness, you will need to show your E111 and some identification, such as a driving licence or passport. Make sure that the doctor treating you knows you have an E111 form. Visitors from outside the EU are advised to take out their own accident and health insurance before travelling or be willing to pay for treatment received.

5 Pharmacies

An extensive range of medical supplies is available over the counter at pharmacies but many medicines can only be obtained with a prescription from a local doctor. If you have, or are likely to have, any special medical needs it is worth having a letter from your own doctor giving the generic name of any medication you might require. There is a late night pharmacy in O'Connell Street (see p61). ✆ *O'Connell's Late Night Pharmacy: 55 O'Connell St, Dublin 1, 01-873 0427*

6 Dentists

For emergency dental treatment you can go to the Dublin Dental Hospital in Lincoln Place. They also have an after-hours answering service giving appropriate information. Conor Gallagher dentist is happy to deal with visitor emergencies. ✆ *Conor Gallagher: Fenian Street, Dublin 2, 01-678 8158*

7 Personal Safety

Street crime does exist in Dublin, as in any capital city, but sensible precautions should be sufficient to keep you out of trouble. Avoid back streets or poorly lit areas at night. Don't carry around obviously expensive equipment, which will draw attention. If you are unlucky enough to be mugged or attacked, inform the police straight away.

8 Theft

To avoid theft, don't leave things unattended in restaurants or galleries. If you have a car, lock everything in the boot (trunk) where it cannot be seen.

9 Lost Property

If you have any property stolen, report it to the police immediately – you cannot make an insurance claim without the police report. The main bus and rail stations have lost property offices.

10 Street Begging

There are quite a lot of homeless people begging in the streets in Dublin, but they are generally unaggressive and it is a personal choice whether you give handouts or not.

Left **The Shelbourne** Right **The Clarence**

^{TOP}10 Luxury Hotels

1 The Merrion
Dublin's finest hotel may seem unimpressive from the outside, but inside it is the embodiment of Georgian elegance, with ornate plasterwork, antiques, Irish fabrics and marble bathrooms. The modern world hasn't been forgotten – there is also a swimming pool, gym and business facilities. ⊗ Merrion St • Map G5 • 01-603 0600 • www. merrionhotel.com • €€€€€

2 The Clarence
This 19th-century building has been spectactularly renovated by the Irish rock band U2, blending wood panelling with cutting edge modern design. Located in the buzzing Temple Bar area (see pp18–19) and overlooking the Liffey, it has fast become one of the most elegant places to stay in the city. ⊗ 6–8 Wellington Quay • Map D4 • 01-407 0800 • www. theclarence.com • €€€€€

3 The Shelbourne
From the moment you enter the wrought-iron canopied entrance to this beautiful hotel, greeted by the liveried doorman, you will be overawed by the grace and charm that have brought loyal customers here since the 19th century. A true Dublin institution. ⊗ 27 St Stephen's Green • Map F6 • 01-676 6471 • €€€€€

4 The Westbury
For 5-star luxury you can't do better than this Grafton Street hotel – the accommodation of choice for politicians and celebrities. It even has its own shopping mall if you can't face the crowds outside. ⊗ Grafton St • Map E5 • 01-679 1122 • www. jurysdoyle.com • €€€€€

5 Berkeley Court
This elegant hotel in traditional style is five minutes by car from the centre. It pampers its, often high-profile, guests from the minute they walk through the door. Standard rooms provide bathrobes and slippers, while executive rooms have stunning four-poster beds. ⊗ Lansdowne Rd • DART Lansdowne Road • 01-660 1711 • www. jurysdoyle.com • €€€€€

6 Four Seasons Hotel
In the prestigious residential district of Ballsbridge, just 10 minutes by car from the city centre, is this luxury chain hotel with all the facilities one might expect: fitness centre and swimming pool, business facilities and 259 well-equipped rooms. A good choice if you want luxury away from the hub of the city. ⊗ Simmonscourt Rd, Ballsbridge • DART Sandymount • 01-665 4000 • €€€€€

7 Conrad International
This recently refurbished and comfortable modern hotel is conveniently situated just around the corner from St Stephen's Green. ⊗ Earlsfort Terrace • Map F6 • 01-676 5555 • www.conraddublin.com • €€€€€

8 Morrison
Given that it was renovated by fashion designer and Dublin resident John Rocha, it is unsurprising that behind the Georgian façade of the Morrison hides an interior of supreme style. White walls, Irish carpets and contemporary art are some of its attractions. ⊗ Ormond Quay • Map D3 • 01-878 2999 • www. morrisonhotel.ie • €€€€€

9 The Fitzwilliam
This award-winning hotel, designed by the Conran partnership, boasts luxurious rooms and the largest roof garden in the country. ⊗ St Stephen's Green • Map F6 • 01-478 7000 • €€€€€

10 The Davenport
Housed in a beautiful Georgian building, the Davenport retains traditional style while offering all modern facilities. Its bar takes the theme of presidents around the world, and is decorated with portraits. ⊗ Merrion Sq • Map G5 • 01-607 3500 • €€€€

Note: Unless otherwise stated, all hotels accept credit cards, have en-suite bathrooms and air conditioning

Streetsmart

Left **Brooks Hotel** Right **Trinity Capital**

🔟 Three- and Four-Star Hotels

1 The Gresham
Conveniently located on bustling O'Connell Street (see p61), Dublin's oldest hotel has recently been refurbished, but Waterford crystal chandeliers still add a touch of 19th-century elegance. 🔍 *O'Connell St • Map F2 • 01-874 6881 • www.gresham.ie • €€€€*

2 Herbert Park
A beautiful modern hotel, with floor to ceiling windows looking out over the surrounding parkland. Contemporary Irish art decorates communal areas, including the lounge and restaurant. 🔍 *Ballsbridge • DART Sandymount • 01-667 2200 • www.herbertparkhotel.ie • €€€€€*

3 Hibernian
For those who prefer quieter surroundings. An elegant, early 20th-century building with very comfortable rooms. 🔍 *Eastmoreland Place, Ballsbridge • Bus No. 10 • 01-668 7666 • www.hibernianhotel.com • €€€€€*

4 The Morgan
All pale walls and beechwood furniture, the Morgan encapsulates the contemporary style of the Temple Bar area with its minimalist design. It can be noisy on the streets, so try for top-floor rooms. 🔍 *Fleet St, Temple Bar • Map E3 • 01-679 3939 • www.themorgan.com • €€€€*

5 The Burlington
A traditional hotel in style with dark wood, chandeliers and chintz fabrics, the Burlington is nevertheless home to Doyle's, a thoroughly modern and lively Irish cabaret featuring song, dance and tall stories. 🔍 *Upper Leeson St • Map F6 • 01-660 5222 • www.jurysdoyle.com • €€€€€*

6 The Schoolhouse
Converted from a 19th-century schoolhouse which saw some action during the Easter Rising (see p31), many original features have been retained at this unusual 4-star hotel. Former classrooms have been converted into a restaurant and bar – fortunately the modern Irish food is far better than school dinners! 🔍 *Northumberland Rd, Ballsbridge • DART Lansdowne Road • 01-667 5014 • €€€€€*

7 Brooks Hotel
With its dark wood foyer and bar and royal blue carpets, Brooks exudes old-world style. Downstairs, however, is Francesca's restaurant, with a more modern decor, reflecting its menu of fine modern Irish food (see p49). Set in a quiet street, the lively pubs and bars around Grafton Street are just minutes away. 🔍 *Drury St • Map E5 • 01-670 4000 • www.sinnotthotels.com • €€€€€*

8 Clarion Hotel Stephens Hall
On the edge of St Stephen's Green, this member of the Clarion hotel chain has been smartly decorated. Not as unusual as some of Dublin's top hotels, but makes for a comfortable and central stay. 🔍 *14–17 Lower Leeson St • Map F6 • 01-638 1111 • www.premgroup.com • €€€€*

9 Chief O'Neills
A wonderful futuristic-style hotel in the renovated Smithfield area. It is named after a 19th-century Irish-born Chicago Chief of Police, Francis O'Neill. Panoramic views of Dublin can be seen from the Smithfield Chimney in front of the hotel (see p66). 🔍 *Smithfield Market • Map C3 • 01-817 3838 • www.chiefoneills.com • €€€€*

10 Trinity Capital
This new hotel overlooking the walls of Trinity College has paid attention to every detail, combining Art Deco influences with a modern twist. Most striking are its oversized lilac sofas in the foyer, and wonderful sculptures. Just in case Dublin goes up in flames, avoid lower level rooms – the hotel is located next to a fire station. Excellent Irish breakfast. 🔍 *Pearse St • Map F4 • 01-648 1000 • www.capital-hotels.com • €€€€*

Left **Harrington Hall** Right **Trinity Lodge**

Townhouse Hotels

1 Browns Hotel
As with most of Dublin's townhouse hotels, Browns has perfectly preserved the Georgian setting, while adding modern facilities, including TVs and writing desks. The result is a blend of comfort and convenience. ◈ *Gardiner St • Map F1 • 855 0034 • www.brownshotelireland. com • €€€*

2 Pembroke Townhouse
Every detail here exudes classic style, yet all the en-suite rooms are fully equipped with modern facilities including cable TV. Traditional Irish breakfast. ◈ *90 Pembroke Rd • Bus No. 10 • 660 0277 • www.pembroke townhouse.ie • Dis. access • €€€*

3 Butlers Townhouse
Each of the 20 rooms here has an individual decor, yet the feel of the place is like a friendly country house, with sofas around the lounge's fireplace. ◈ *Lansdowne Rd • DART Lansdowne Road • 667 4022 • www. butlers-hotels.com • Dis. access €€€€*

4 Harrington Hall
A collection of Georgian houses were combined together in 1998 to provide 28 meticulous rooms. The Irish breakfast is an excellent start to a day of sightseeing, and there is a private car park behind the hotel, which is always a bonus in congested Dublin. ◈ *Harcourt St • Map F5 • 475 3497 • www.harringtonhall.com • Dis. access • €€€€*

5 Longfields Hotel
A relaxing place to stay, with impeccable service. It is decorated with period features such as chandeliers and original plasterwork. ◈ *Fitzwilliam St • Map E6 • 676 1367 • www. longfieldshotel.ie • Dis. access • €€€€*

6 Trinity Lodge
The 15 rooms of this Georgian townhouse are all elegantly decorated and fully equipped, while the communal rooms benefit from antique furniture. ◈ *12 Frederick St • Map F5 • 679 5044 • www.trinitylodge.com • €€€–€€€€*

7 Anglesea Townhouse
Just 10 minutes' from the city centre by car, this early 20th-century house has been adapted into a small hotel with seven rooms. The breakfastis superb. ◈ *Anglesea Rd • DART Sandymount • 668 3877 • €€€*

8 Belcamp Hutchinson
This impressive 18th-century family mansion is still privately owned, which is apparent in its loving renovation into a plush hotel, combining traditional style with all modern amenities. Golf and horse-riding are available nearby if you're looking for outdoor activity. The city centre is 15 minutes' and the airport 10 minutes' drive away. ◈ *Balgriffin • Bus No. 42 • 846 0843 • www.belcamphutchinson. com • €€€*

9 Baggot Court
A short walk from St Stephen's Green and the shopping hub of the city on Grafton Street, this converted Georgian townhouse makes an unusual but attractive place to stay, as well as an affordable one. The price includes a full Irish breakfast. Smokers should be aware that the whole establishment is non-smoking. ◈ *Lower Baggot St • Map F6 • 661 2819 • €€€*

10 Hotel St George
The period staircase in this converted Georgian house is one of its most striking features, as well as the glistening crystal chandeliers made from Waterford glass *(see p83)*. The hotel is conveniently situated for all the literary sights north of the Liffey such as the Dublin Writers' Museum *(see p62)*, so it is an ideal place for book lovers. ◈ *Parnell Sq • Map E1 • 874 5611 • Dis. access • €€€*

Note: *Unless otherwise stated, all hotels accept credit cards, have en-suite bathrooms and air conditioning*

Streetsmart

130

Price Categories

For a standard, double room per night (with breakfast if included), taxes and extra charges.

€	under €50
€€	€50–100
€€€	€100–150
€€€€	€150–200
€€€€€	over €200

Above **Number 31**

🔟 Guesthouses

1 Number 31
This unique hotel compries two coach houses (converted by Irish architect Sam Stephenson in 1958) connected by private gardens to a classic Georgian house. With just 21 guestrooms it's a lovely place to stay, not least because all of Dublin's sights are within walking distance. ◈ *31 Leeson Close* • Map F6 • *676 5011* • €€€€

2 Cedar Lodge
Opposite the British Embassy and RDS grounds, this 4-star guesthouse provides all the comforts of home. ◈ *98 Merrion Rd, Ballsbridge* • DART Sandymount, Bus Nos. 7, 8, 45 • *668 4410* • €€€

3 Raglan Lodge
A privately owned, converted Victorian house, set in the heart of Ballsbridge's elegant residential district. Guests are encouraged to relax together in front of the fire in the lounge, but the bedrooms are comfortable and stylish if you're feeling less sociable. ◈ *Raglan Rd, Ballsbridge* • DART Sandymount • *660 6697* • €€€

4 Albany House
This 18th-century house was once owned by the Earl of Clonmel, but is now privately run as a comfortable hotel, cleverly blending period furnishings with modern amenities. ◈ *Harcourt St* • Map E5 • *475 1092* • €€€

5 Brownes Townhouse
If you want a treat in the heart of the city, head for this boutique hotel, once home to the Earl of Shelbourne. The brasserie is also celebrated. ◈ *22 St Stephen's Green* • Map E6 • *01-638 3939* • www.brownesdublin.com • €€€€€

6 Waterloo House
This 4-star guesthouse is family-run and offers 17 fully equipped bedrooms in its three-storey Georgian house. It also benefits from a private car park, which is useful as the city centre is 10 minutes' drive away. ◈ *Waterloo Rd, Ballsbridge* • DART Lansdowne Road • *660 1888* • Dis. access • €€€

7 King Sitric
Better known as a fabulous fish restaurant *(see p77)*, the King Sitric has recently branched out into hotel accommodation, with eight beautiful guestrooms, all charmingly named after local lighthouses and overlooking the sea. Enjoy the bustle of the city by day, then return to this haven of seaside calm. ◈ *East Pier, Howth* • DART Howth • *832 5235* • www.kingsitric.ie • Dis. access • €€€€

8 The Fitzwilliam
In the heart of Georgian Dublin, close to St Stephen's Green, this spacious townhouse has lots of charm and all the necessary mod cons. Friendly and relaxed, there are 13 en-suite rooms. ◈ *41 Fitzwilliam St* • Map H6 • *01-662 5155* • fitzwilliamguesthouse@ ericom.ie • €€

9 Eglinton Manor
This imposing, 19th-century listed building is a wonderful place to stay, with eight guestrooms and an executive suite, all lovingly decorated with Irish crafts. There's a beautiful marble fireplace to gather around in the lounge on cold winter nights, or, in summer, enjoy a round of golf or a horse ride, both available nearby. ◈ *Eglinton Rd, Donnybrook* • Bus Nos. 10, 11, 11A, 11B • *269 3273* • €€€

10 Comfort Inn
Excellent value for money right in the heart of the city. Pale floors, bright red sofas and a welcoming fire make up the lounge area, and the bedrooms are stylishly decorated too. The small garden at the back of the hotel is a wonderful and relaxing bonus in good weather. ◈ *Talbot St* • Map F2 • *01-874 9202* • www.comfort-inn-dublin.com • Dis. access *(family rooms)* • €€€–€€€€

Left **Waterford Castle** Right **Hunters Hotel gardens**

TOP 10 Waterford and Limerick Hotels

1 The K Club

The K Club is a 5-star hotel and abounds in activities. There are two 18-hole championship golf courses designed by Arnold Palmer, one of which is the venue for the Ryder Cup in 2006. River fishing is also available. Rooms are luxurious, with all modern conveniences. ✪ *Straffan, Co Kildare • Map P5 • 01-601 7200 • www.kclub.ie • Dis. access • €€€€€*

2 Mount Juliet Estate

This 1,500-acre estate boasts an 18-hole golf course designed by Jack Nicklaus which hosted the WGC American Express Championship in 2002. There is also a spa and facilities for archery, clay pigeon shooting and horse-riding. Inside, the rooms are stunning and the two restaurants are award-winners. ✪ *Thomastown, Co Kilkenny • Map P5 • 056 777 3000 • www.mountjuliet.com • Dis. access • €€€€€*

3 Hunter's Hotel

One of the oldest coaching inns in Ireland, the Hunter's Hotel offers gardens, golf, tennis, horse-riding and fishing. Beaches are nearby and the restaurant takes advantage of the fresh fish for its traditional Irish cooking. ✪ *Rathnew, Co Wicklow • Map N5 • 0404 40106 • www.hunters.ie • Dis. access • €€€€*

4 Rathsallagh House

Once named the Country House of the Year, Rathsallagh House has an 18-hole championship golf course and is set on 530 lush acres of rolling landscape with several lakes, streams and woodland. On the west side of the Wicklow Mountains. ✪ *Dunlavin, Co Wicklow • Map N5 • 045 403112 • www.rathsallagh.com • Dis. access • €€€€€*

5 Waterford Castle

One of the unique hotel experiences in the world. The 15th-century castle is set on a 300-acre island overlooking the River Suir. Access is by car ferry only and the hotel offers the very highest standards of comfort, luxuriously furnished with antiques and open fireplaces. ✪ *Ballinakill, Waterford • Map Q5 • 051 878203 • www.waterfordcastle.com • €€€€€*

6 Adare Manor Hotel

Situated in one of the prettiest villages in the country, this 18th-century manor house is now a 5-star luxury hotel. Once the seat of the Earls of Dunraven, it is now American-owned. Good service is guaranteed. ✪ *Main St, Adare Village, Co Limerick • Map P3 • 061 396566 • www.adaremanor.com • €€€€€*

7 Butler House

Perhaps the most luxurious stay in Kilkenny. This Georgian townhouse overlooks the river and Kilkenny Castle. Rooms are spacious, and sweeping staircases lead down to the well-maintained gardens. ✪ *15–16 Patrick St, Kilkenny • Map P4 • 056 776 5707 • www.butler.ie • €€€€*

8 Legends Townhouse

This bed-and-breakfast provides a warm Irish welcome. The restaurant offers excellent cuisine and fine wines. ✪ *The Kiln, Cashel, Co Tipperary • Map P4 • 062 61292 • www.legendsguesthouse.com • €€€*

9 Richmond House

This 18th-century Georgian country house offers an award-winning restaurant and stunning grounds. Log fires warm the rooms, which have period features. ✪ *Cappoquin, Co Waterford • Map P5 • 058 54278 • www.richmondhouse.net • €€€*

10 Hanora's Cottage

The Comeragh Mountains near here offer walking trails. Work up an appetite to enjoy the Irish cuisine of the restaurant. There is also a hot tub. ✪ *Nire Valley, Ballymacarbry, Co Waterford • Map Q4 • 052 36134 • hanorascottage@eircom.net • €€€*

Note: *Unless otherwise stated, all hotels accept credit cards, have en-suite bathrooms and air conditioning*

Price Categories

For a standard, double room per night (with breakfast if included), taxes and extra charges.

€ under €50
€€ €50–€100
€€€ €100–€150
€€€€ €150–€200
€€€€€ over €200

Above **Ashford Castle restaurant**

🔟 Galway and Connemara Hotels

1 Ashford Castle
This glorious castle is now a 5-star hotel and resort. Facilities include a health club with steam room, sauna and whirlpool. Available on the resort are golf, horse-riding, falconry, cruising and fishing on Lough Corrib. ◊ *Cong, Co. Mayo • Map M2 • 094 954 6003 • www.ashford.ie • Dis. access • €€€€€*

2 Delphi Lodge
One of Ireland's most famous fishing lodges. The atmosphere is elegant but informal, with a library, a billiards room and a large drawing room overlooking the lake. Five restored cottages provide further accommodation. The surroundings are home to abundant wildlife, including falcons, badgers and otters. Fly-fishing offered for salmon. ◊ *Leenane, Co. Galway • Map N2 • 095 42222 • www. delphilodge.ie • €€€€*

3 Ballynahinch Castle
Once home to the pirate queen Grace O'Malley *(see p106)*, this casually elegant 4-star hotel enjoys a breathtaking location, ringed by the Twelve Bens Mountains. The restaurant serves fresh game and fish. ◊ *Ballynahinch, Recess, Connemara, Co. Galway • Map M2 • 095 31006 • www.ballynahinch-castle.com • €€€€–€€€€€*

4 Cashel House
An oasis of calm in the wilderness of the Atlantic coast, this hotel rests elegantly amid beautiful gardens. Rooms look onto the gardens or the sea. Antiques and period paintings abound, as do open turf fires. Private beach. Walks, cycling, horse-riding and fishing are available. ◊ *Cashel, Co. Galway • Map N2 • 095 31001 • www.cashel-house-hotel .com • €€€€€*

5 Erriseask House Hotel
Ten minutes' drive from Clifden, this small modern hotel on the shores of Mannin Bay is near the beach. If long walks amid Connemara's coastal scenery don't draw you here, the excellent restaurant should. ◊ *Ballyconneely, Clifden, Co. Galway • Map M1 • 095 23553 • www. erriseask.com • €€€*

6 Currarevagh House
This country mansion, dated 1842, is situated right beside Lough Corrib in private woodland. Absorb the splendid isolation by walking in the woods, or taking out one of the fishing boats. The house has a tennis court, and golf and riding are locally available. ◊ *Oughterard, Connemara, Co. Galway • Map M2 • 091 552312 • www. currarevagh.com • €€€€*

7 Rock Glen Manor House
This shooting lodge on the shores of Ardbear Bay enjoys spectacular views. Horse-riding, fishing and walking available. ◊ *Clifden, Connemara, Co. Galway • Map M1 • 095 21035 • www.connemara.net/ rockglen-hotel • €€€€–€€€€€*

8 Olde Railway Hotel
The town of Westport is the wildest of the wild west. This 18th-century coaching inn has a homely feel, with turf fires and antique furniture. ◊ *The Mall, Westport, Co. Mayo • Map M2 • 098 25166 • www.theolderailwayhotel .com • €€€*

9 Jury's Inn Galway
The Jury's chain offers good value well-placed accommodation. This branch is located beside the historic Spanish Arch overlooking Galway Bay. ◊ *Quay St, Galway • Map N2 • 091 566444 • www. jurysdoyle.com • Dis. access • €€€*

10 Ballinalacken Castle Country House
The ruins of Ballinalacken Castle are right beside this guesthouse. The restaurant serves food by award-winning chef Frank Sheedy. ◊ *Coast Rd, Doolin, Co Clare • Map N2 • 065 707 4025 • www. ballinalackencastle.com • €€€*

Left **Sheen Falls Lodge** Right **The Park Hotel**

🔟 Cork and Kerry Hotels

1 The Park Hotel
This hotel is in a 19th-century limestone building. Enjoy the restaurant's mix of classic and progressive cooking, while looking out over the 11-acre garden and Kenmare Bay. The hotel has a spa and is adjacent to an 18-hole golf course; salmon fishing and riding are available nearby. Ⓢ Kenmare, Co Kerry • Map Q2 • 064 41200 • www.parkkenmare.com • Dis. access • €€€€€

2 Sheen Falls Lodge
This rambling lodge is situated on a dramatic 300-acre estate above Sheen Falls and Kenmare Bay. The award-winning restaurant, La Cascade, overlooks a waterfall. The lodge has a fitness centre, swimming pool, billiards room and wine cellar. Ⓢ Kenmare, Co Kerry • Map Q2 • 064 41600 • www.sheenfallslodge.ie • Dis. access • €€€€€

3 Ballymaloe House
This ivy-covered Georgian guesthouse on a 400-acre farm is the best in its category. Enjoy the simply prepared food from the award-winning restaurant. Or try your hand at the small golf course, tennis court or splash around in the outdoor pool. Fishing and riding can be arranged. Ⓢ Shanagarry, Midleton, Co Cork • Map Q3 • 021 465 2531 • www.ballymaloe.ie • Dis. access • €€€€€

4 Coolclogher House
Set in 60 acres of parkland, Coolclogher House is within walking distance of Killarney National Park. The large guestrooms have lovely views. The Victorian conservatory is built around a huge specimen camellia over 170 years old. Ⓢ Mill Rd, Killarney, Co Kerry • Map Q2 • 064 35996 • www. coolclogher house.com • €€€€

5 The Old Bank House
Facing the bustling harbour, these two Georgian townhouses have been voted one of the "Top 100 places to stay in Ireland" every year since 1990. Ⓢ 11 Pearse St, Kinsale, Co Cork • Map Q3 • 021 477 4075 • www. oldbankhousekinsale.com • Dis. access • €€€€

6 Doyle's Seafood Bar and Townhouse
This cosy guesthouse in Dingle town is also one of the best loved restaurants in Ireland. Lobster, the speciality, is chosen from a tank in the bar and the menu features the catch of the day. A red exterior hints at the warmth within: stone and wood decor, and an old range in the kitchen. Self-catering apartments are also available. Ⓢ John St, Dingle, Co Kerry • Map Q1 • 066 915 1174 • www. doylesofdingle.com • €€€

7 Darby O'Gill's
This friendly family-run hotel is in a quiet rural setting five minutes' drive from Killarney town. Families are particularly well catered for. Traditional Irish music is played nightly in the summer. Ⓢ Lissivigeen, Mallow Rd, Killarney, Co Kerry • Map Q2 • 064 34168 • darbyogill @tinet.ie • €€–€€€

8 Aherne's Townhouse
This family-run pub is also a hotel and restaurant. The sitting room has an open fire and lots of books. The rooms are decorated with antiques, and some have balconies. Ⓢ 163 N Main St, Youghal, Co Cork • Map Q4 • 024 92424 • www.ahernes.com • Dis. access • €€€€

9 Shelburne Lodge
Once the home of Lord Shelburne (1737–1805), former prime minister of Great Britain. Informal, with log fire and wood floors. Ⓢ Killowen, Cork Rd, Kenmare, Co Kerry • Map Q2 • 064 41013 • www.kenmare.net/ shelburne • €€€

10 Muckross Park Hotel
Set in Killarney National Park, this plush Victorian hotel incorporates an award-winning restaurant and Molly Darcy's pub. Ⓢ Muckross Village, Killarney, Co Kerry • Map Q2 • 064 31938 • www.muckross park.com • €€€€€

Note: Unless otherwise stated, all hotels accept credit cards, have en-suite bathrooms and air conditioning

Above **Streeve Hill gardens**

Price Categories

For a standard, double room per night (with breakfast if included), taxes and extra charges.

€	under €50
€€	€50–€100
€€€	€100–€150
€€€€	€150–€200
€€€€€	over €200

⑩ Northwest and Northern Hotels

1 Coopershill
Set on a 500-acre estate of farm and woodland, this Georgian mansion lets you forget the world outside. Elegance is a virtue here, with candle-lit dinners served with the family silver. Along with the open log fires there are modern comforts, and peacocks wander through the garden. ⊗ *Riverstown, Co Sligo • Map L3 • 071 916 5108 • ohara@ coopershill.com • Dis. access • €€€€*

2 Temple House
The Perceval family have owned the house since 1665; the current building was refurbished in 1864. Rooms have a traditional atmosphere with log fires and canopied beds. The area has many archaeological sights and the hotel can advise on walks. ⊗ *Bally-mote, Co Sligo • Map L3 • 071 918 3329 • www. templehouse.ie • €€€*

3 Rathmullan Country House
Located on the quiet shores of Donegal, this country house also has award-winning gardens. Rooms are decorated in period style and family rooms and suites are available. There is an indoor swimming pool, steam room and tennis courts for added luxury. ⊗ *Rathmullan, Co Donegal • Map K4 • 074 915 8188 • www.rathmullanhouse. com • €€€€*

4 Ardnamona
The surrounding natural beauty of Ardna-mona is complemented by the glorious wild gardens planted in the 1880s and now a National Heritage Site. Rooms are spacious and modern with great views. ⊗ *Lough Eske, Co Donegal • Map K4 • 074 972 2650 • www.ardnamona.ie • €€€*

5 Cromleach Lodge Country House
The lodge's unconventional design makes the most of the view overlooking Lough Arrow and the Bricklieve Mountains. A patio catches the sun and rooms all have great views, with a semi-traditional decor. There is a piano bar for the use of residents. ⊗ *Castle-baldwin, Co Sligo • Map L3 • 071 916 5155 • www. cromleach.com • €€€€€*

6 Bushmills Inn
Once you check into this old coaching inn and mill house, you may find it difficult to leave. Not only will the open peat fires, pitched pine and gas lights make you want to stay, the Bushmills distillery – the oldest in Northern Ireland – in the village may make you forget how to get home. Golfing and fishing available nearby. ⊗ *9 Dunluce Rd, Bushmills, Co Antrim • Map K5 • 028 2073 2339 • www. bushmillsinn.com • Dis. access • €€€€*

7 The Crescent Townhouse
The chic end of Belfast's hotel market. There is a highly rated on-site brasserie and it is just a short walk to the Golden Mile. ⊗ *13 Lower Crescent, Belfast • Map L6 • 028 9032 3349 • www. crescenttownhouse.com • €€*

8 Tyrella House
At the foot of the Mourne Mountains, Tyrella hides behind tall beech woods. Horse-riding and fishing can be arranged. ⊗ *Downpatrick, Co, Down • Map L6 • 028 44 851422 • tyrella.corbett @virgin.net • €€*

9 Streeve Hill
Most visitors here are on a tour of the Antrim coast and the breakfast at Streeve Hill will set you on your way. Rooms vary, from cosy rooms with a shower to a large room with side bedroom, ideal for children. ⊗ *Limavady, Co Londonderry • Map K5 • 028 777 66563 • pandj welsh@yahoo.co.uk • €€*

10 Charlemont Arms
This modern inn attracts locals as well as visitors to its café/wine bar, one of the best in Armagh. Armagh's two cathedrals are nearby. ⊗ *57–65 English St, Armagh • Map L5 • 028 3752 2028 • www. charlemontarmshotel.com • Dis. access • €€*

General Index

Acknowledgements

Main Contributors

Polly Phillimore has worked as a freelance writer and editor for a number of years and with Dorling Kindersley for seven years. She moved to Ireland from the UK in 1995 and divides her time between Dublin and the West of Ireland.

Award-winning travel writer Andrew Sanger has contributed to a variety of newspapers, magazines and travel websites. From 1990–99 he was the editor of Rail Europe magazine, and is the author of more than 20 guidebooks, mainly on Ireland, France and Israel.

Produced by Sargasso Media Ltd, London

Project Editor Zoë Ross
Art Editors Philip Lord, Janis Utton
Picture Research Monica Allende
Proofreader Stewart J Wild
Indexer Hilary Bird
Editorial Assistance Nonie Luke

Additional Contributors
Robin Gauldie, Jason Mitchell, Christina Park
Main Photographer Magnus Rew
Additional Photography
Joe Cornish, Tim Daly, Anthony Souter, Clive Streeter, Alan Williams
Illustrator Chris Orr & Associates

FOR DORLING KINDERSLEY
Publishing Managers Jane Ewart, Fay Franklin
Publisher Douglas Amrine
Cartography Co-ordinator Casper Morris
DTP Jason Little
Production Melanie Dowland

Maps James Macdonald, Rob Clynes (Mapping Ideas Ltd)

Picture Credits
t-top; tc-top centre; tr-top right; cla-centre left above; ca-centre above; cra-centre right above; cl-centre left; c-centre; cr-centre right; clb-centre left below; cb-centre below; crb-centre right below; bl-below left; bc-below centre; br-below right.

Every effort has been made to trace the copyright holders, and we apologize in advance for any unintentional omissions. We would be pleased to insert the appropriate acknowledgements in any subsequent edition of this publication. The publishers would like to thank the following individuals, companies, and picture libraries for permission to reproduce their photographs:

AKG, London: 34b

BRIDGEMAN ART LIBRARY: Private Collection "*The Death of Cuchulain*" c.1940 by John Yunge-Bateman 38b, The Fine Art Society 38t; Courtesy of BROOKS HOTEL: 48b; CHESTER BEATTY LIBRARY, DUBLIN: 16tl, 16tr, 16b, 17t, 17b;

COLLECTIONS: Michael Diggin 75tr, Image Ireland 134tr, Mark O'Sullivan 34tl, 41tr, George Wright 37tl; CORBIS: 1, 31cla, 50–51, 110–111, 118–119; Courtesy of DART: /AFAomeara 121tr; Courtesy of DUBLIN BUS: 121 tl; MARY EVANS PICTURE LIBRARY: Jeffrey Morgan 35tl; GUINNESS STOREHOUSE: © 2002 Fennell Photography 24cb, 24b, 25t, 25cr, 25b, 76tr; HULTON ARCHIVE: 30tr

IMAGEFILE, Dublin: 28–9, 64–5, 72–3, 80tl, 80tr, 80b, 81b, 117t; IRELAND BLUE BOOK: 77t, 85t, 97t, 103t, 107t

NATIONAL GALLERY OF IRELAND: "*The Piping Boy*" by Nathaniel Hone the Elder 6bl, 12–13, © Michael Yeats "*The Liffey Swim*" by Jack B Yeats 12b, "*The Marriage of Strongbow and Aoife*" by Daniel Maclise 13t, "*Christ in the House of Martha and Mary*" by Rubens 13cr, © ADAGP, Paris and DACS, London 2002 "*River Scene, Autumn*" by Monet 13b PA: 30tl, 31tr, 37tr

RETROGRAPH: 7cr, 24-25; REX FEATURES: 35tr, 35br; © 2001 SHEEN FALLS LODGE: 134tl; TOPHAM PICTUREPOINT: 31b

All other images are © DK. For further information see www.dkimages.com

DK publishes a wide range of guidebooks, including nearly 20 in this Eyewitness Top Ten series and more than 70 in the award-winning Eyewitness Travel Guide series. To see our complete range of guides, phrasebooks and maps, visit us at **www.dk.com**

Dorling Kindersley Special Editions

Dorling Kindersley books can be purchased in bulk quantities at discounted prices for use in promotions or as premiums. We are also able to offer special editions and personalized jackets, corporate imprints, and excerpts from all of our books, tailored specifically to meet your own needs.

To find out more, please contact: (in the United Kingdom) – Sarah.Burgess@dk.com or Special Sales, Dorling Kindersley Limited, 80 Strand, London WC2R 0RL; (in the United States) – Special Markets Department, DK Publishing, Inc., 375 Hudson Street, New York, New York 10014.

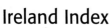

Ireland Index